Journey Through the BIBL

D0989214

Dr. Justo González, writer of this study resource, was born in Havana, Cuba, the son of two Methodist ministers. He completed his S.T.B. at Union Theological Seminary in Matanzas, Cuba, and then came to the United States to pursue graduate studies in theology. He obtained his Ph.D. in historical theology from Yale University. Since that time, he has held teaching positions at the Evangelical Seminary of Puerto Rico and Candler School of Theology. Although he now teaches on an occasional basis, he is a full-time writer and lecturer.

His books, originally written in either Spanish or English, have been translated into several other languages. He has also written numerous United Methodist curriculum materials as well as materials for other denominations.

JOURNEY THROUGH THE BIBLE: ACTS. An official resource for The United Methodist Church prepared by the General Board of Discipleship through Church School Publications and published quarterly by Cokesbury, The United Methodist Publishing House; 201 Eighth Avenue, South; P.O. Box 801; Nashville, TN 37202-0801. Printed in the United States of America. Copyright ©1995 by Cokesbury. All rights reserved.

Scripture quotations in this publication, unless otherwise indicated, are from the New Revised Standard Version of the Bible, copyright ©1989 by the Division of Christian Education of the National Council of the Churches of Christ in the United States of America, and are used by permission. All rights reserved.

For information concerning permission to reproduce any material in this publication, call 615-749-6421, or write to Cokesbury, Permissions Office, P.O. Box 801, Nashville, TN 37202-0801.

To order copies of this publication, call toll free 800-672-1789. Call Monday–Friday 7:00–6:30 Central Time; 5:00–4:30 Pacific Time; Saturday, 9:00–5:00. You may FAX your order to 800-445-8189. Telecommunication Device for the Deaf/Telex Telephone: 800-227-4091. Automated order system is available after office hours. Use your Cokesbury account, American Express, Visa, Discover, or MasterCard.

EDITORIAL TEAM
Debra G. Ball-Kilbourne,
  Editor
Linda H. Leach,
  Assistant Editor
Linda O. Spicer,
  Adult Section
  Assistant

DESIGN TEAM
Susan J. Scruggs,
  Design Supervisor,
  Cover Design
Teresa B. Travelstead,
  Layout Designer

ADMINISTRATIVE STAFF
Neil M. Alexander,
  Vice-President,
  Publishing
Duane A. Ewers,
  Editor of Church
  School Publications
Gary L. Ball-Kilbourne,
  Executive Editor of
  Adult Publications

Art: Charles Shaw,
  pp. 6, 7
  Marvine Gardner,
  p. 111

Cokesbury

TABLE OF CONTENTS

Volume 13: Acts   by Justo L. González

2		INTRODUCTION TO THE SERIES
3	Chapter 1	TONGUES
11	Chapter 2	AUTHORITY
19	Chapter 3	CONFLICT
28	Chapter 4	POWER
36	Chapter 5	CONVERSION
44	Chapter 6	HORIZONS
52	Chapter 7	JEALOUSY AND JOY
60	Chapter 8	JERUSALEM
68	Chapter 9	ATHENS
76	Chapter 10	CORINTH
84	Chapter 11	EPHESUS
92	Chapter 12	TRIAL
100	Chapter 13	SHIPWRECK
109		ACTS 29?

12 13 14 15 - 25 24 23 22

ᝒNTRODUCTION TO THE SERIES

Welcome to JOURNEY THROUGH THE BIBLE!
You are about to embark on an adventure that can change
your life.

WHAT TO BRING WITH YOU

Don't worry about packing much for your trip. All you need to bring with
you on this journey are
- an openness to God speaking to you in the words of Scripture
- companions to join you on the way, and
- your Bible

ITINERARY

In each session of this volume of JOURNEY THROUGH THE BIBLE, first you
will be offered some hints for what to look for as you read the Bible text,
and then you will be guided through four "dimensions" of study. Each is
intended to help you through a well-rounded appreciation and application
of the Bible's words.

HOW TO PREPARE FOR YOUR JOURNEY THROUGH THE BIBLE

Although you will gain much if all you do is show up for Bible study and par-
ticipate willingly in the session, you can do a few things to gain even more:
- Read in advance the Bible passage mentioned in What to Watch For,
  using the summaries and hints as you read.
- During your Bible reading, answer the questions in Dimension 1.
- Read the rest of the session in this study book.
- Try a daily discipline of reading the Bible passages suggested in
  Dimension 4. Note that the Bible texts listed in Dimension 4 do *not* relate
  to a particular session. But if you continue with this daily discipline, by
  the end of thirteen weeks, you will have read through *all* of that portion
  of the Bible covered by this volume.

Studying the Bible is a lifelong project. JOURNEY THROUGH THE BIBLE
provides you with a guided tour for a few of the steps along your way. May
God be with you on your journey!

Gary L. Ball-Kilbourne
Executive Editor, Adult Publications
Church School Publications

Questions or comments?
Call Curric-U-Phone 1-800-251-8591

Acts
2:1-13

1

*T*ONGUES

What to Watch For

This first lesson is both an introduction to the Book of Acts as well as a
study of a particular passage.

In **general**, as you read Acts, watch for these emphases:
➤ It is directly connected to the Gospel of Luke.
➤ Like Luke, its companion piece, Acts indicates a significant interest in
all of humankind.
➤ As was the case in Luke, Acts focuses on the role of women in the
mission of the church.
➤ The Book of Acts is interested in how the church brought in those who
would otherwise be outsiders and what the church learned from doing
so.
➤ The writer of Acts was attentive to such details as titles of officials,
places, and so forth.
➤ Despite attention to details, the writer of Acts left many gaps in the
story, sometimes leaving us wondering about the connection between
the various stories.

In **particular**, watch for this emphasis in the passage we study in this
session:
➤ The reactions of the various people highlighted in the story.

3

1. Although it is not part of the passage we are studying, you may wish to read Acts 1:1-2, comparing it with Luke 1:1-4. What does this tell us about the relationship between the two books?

2. The passage says that "they were all together" (1). Who is meant by "all"?

3. How did various people in the story react?

4. Who spoke in various languages? Who heard?

5. How did those who heard react?

A SINGLE WORK IN TWO VOLUMES

Volume 1: The Gospel of Luke
Since many have undertaken to set down an orderly account of the events that have been fulfilled among us, . . . I too decided, after investigating everything carefully from the very first, to write an orderly account for you, most excellent Theophilus (1:1, 3).

Volume 2: The Book of Acts
In the first book, Theophilus, I wrote about all that Jesus did and taught from the beginning . . . (1:1).

HAVE YOU EVER NOTICED?

Although we often think of Paul as the most prolific writer of the New Testament, that honor in fact corresponds to Luke. In the Bible I am using, Luke and Acts take up sixty-three pages, while the entire body of Pauline letters, from Romans to Philemon, takes up sixty-two pages. Since my New Testament has 243 pages, this means that Luke wrote more than a fourth of the entire New Testament!

Written in a Time of Great Unrest

Acts is the second volume of a two-volume work: Luke/Acts. The two were probably written at about the same time or with very little time in between. Thus, when we read Acts we are reading a document that was probably written around the year A.D. 80. These were not easy times for the Christian church. About fifteen years earlier, Nero had unleashed the first persecution against Christians on the part of Roman authorities. Although things had eased a bit by the time Acts was written, Christians had to walk carefully lest Roman authorities begin actively persecuting them again. To make matters worse, just after Nero's persecution, a great Jewish rebellion had broken out in Judea. The Romans crushed the rebellion mercilessly, destroying much of Jerusalem and the Temple with it. The last remnants of the Christian community in Jerusalem had fled to Pella, where this Jewish Christian church continued its existence for generations. (By A.D. 135, some of them would have returned to Jerusalem.) At the same time, Christianity had expanded throughout the Roman Empire and perhaps even beyond, so that what had begun as a small Jewish sect was now mostly a Gentile movement.

Thus, when Luke wrote the Book of Acts he was looking in various directions at the same time. He was looking at the Roman Empire and its authorities, who often regarded Christianity with suspicion. In this direction, his task was to show that Christianity was not the subversive movement some thought it was. He was also looking at a decreasing, but still powerful, contingent of Jewish Christians who were not altogether sure that it was a good thing for Christianity to have become mostly a Gentile religion. In this regard, his task was to show that the Gentile expansion of Christianity, and the changes it brought, were the work of the Spirit. Finally, Luke was looking at Christians who might waver in times of difficulty. He had to strengthen this group in their resolve, partially by reminding them that Christianity was brought to them at high cost and that they were the heirs of those who suffered for the sake of Christ.

5

The Feast of Pentecost

The particular passage of interest, Acts 2:1-13, is well known. It is the story of what we usually call *Pentecost*. In the Christian calendar, the *Feast of Pentecost* is the day we celebrate the coming of the Holy Spirit upon the newborn church. Originally, however, and certainly when Luke used that name in the Book of Acts, *Pentecost* was a Jewish feast day. In your studies of the Old Testament (the Hebrew Scriptures) you may have come across the term *Feast of Weeks*. It was called that because it took place a *week of weeks* (7 x 7 = 49) after Passover. Since this made it the fiftieth day, Greek-speaking Jews began calling that feast *Pentecost*, from a Greek word meaning "fiftieth."

Read Leviticus 23:15-21, where these observances are prescribed.

New Meaning Given to a Jewish Festival

It was on the day of this Jewish festival that the followers of Jesus were gathered. Since they were all Jews, it was natural for them to observe this day as holy. And, when the tremendous events told here took place on the Day of Pentecost, it was natural for Christians to give a new meaning to that feast day. To this day what we Christians celebrate on Pentecost is the outpouring of the Spirit on the church.

The text says that "they were all together in one place." It is not altogether clear who is meant by "all." Since Luke had just told of the election of Matthias to be the twelfth apostle, it is natural to think that "all" means all twelve apostles. As you read the first and second chapters of Acts, however, you will note that, even in the story of the election of Matthias, there were about 120 persons. You will also note that, in explaining what is taking place, Peter quoted a passage from Joel that says "your sons and your daughters shall prophesy" (17). This would make little sense if there were only twelve men speaking. Therefore, it seems likely that in saying that "they were all together" Luke intended to include all the disciples who were in Jerusalem.

The story is well known. While all these people were gathered together, there were some portentous events—a great sound and tongues "as of fire" resting on each of those present. Then "*all of them* [italics added] were filled with the Holy Spirit and began to speak in other languages, as the Spirit gave them ability" (4).

WHAT'S IN A WORD?

The word that the New Revised Standard Version of the Bible translates as "languages" is the same word used for the "tongues" of fire. Other translations, such as the King James Version and the Revised Standard Version, use *tongues* in both cases. Do you think that Luke might have purposefully tried to make a connection between the "tongues of fire" and the "tongues" the disciples spoke?

Witnesses to the Events

There is a pause in the narration to tell us of other witnesses to these events. Like all people in this story, the other witnesses were also Jews. They had come from a great variety of places, in every direction from Jerusalem: Parthia, Media, Elam, Mesopotamia, Judea itself, Cappadocia, Pontus, Asia (meaning the Roman province by that name), Phrygia, Pamphylia, Egypt, Libya, Rome, Crete, and Arabia. Apparently, although they were Jews, they spoke a wide variety of languages. And they heard their own languages being spoken!

What Does This Mean?

Up to this point, we had not been told what languages the disciples spoke—except that they were "other languages." Now we have learned that these were not just any languages; they were the languages that would make it possible for all of these hearers to hear in their "own native language."

These various people were obviously amazed! Who would not be? They said to one another, "What does this mean?" Does that surprise you? Apparently all these people could communicate with each other, quite apart from the miracle of Pentecost. Historically, that is precisely how things were. Over

7

You may want to read Acts 1:8. In doing so, you will see that Jesus had promised the gift of the Spirit so that his followers could be witnesses. That is precisely what happened. The disciples received the Spirit and were thereby empowered to witness to all these various people, each in their own native tongue.

the centuries, the Jewish people had been dispersed far and wide. In general, those who lived west of Jerusalem spoke the language of the place where they lived as well as Greek, which had become the common language of trade and government. Those who lived east of Jerusalem, generally spoke, besides their native tongue, Aramaic. (By this time Hebrew was a dead language.) Those who lived in Jerusalem and the nearby areas spoke Aramaic as their native language. Thus, most of these people could communicate among themselves in either Greek or Aramaic, even though most would have other native tongues.

Dimension 3:
What Does the Bible Mean to Us?

Surprising, Awesome, Terrifying Power

Our passage is so well known that we may lose sight of its awesome power. Therefore, before we attempt to apply it to our lives, it may be well to read it again. Read it as if you did not know what is going to happen next. Read it, imagining you were there. Read it, letting it surprise you at every turn.

First of all, remember that for these early disciples the word *Pentecost* had nothing or very little to do with the events with which we associate it today. It was a religious festival. Those who gathered to celebrate it were a community of faithful Jews who believed in Jesus as the Christ—that is, the Messiah. Jesus had promised the gift of the Spirit, but he had said nothing about when this would be granted, nor about how it would manifest itself.

People were gathered for a religious celebration. *Suddenly*, that is, *most unexpectedly*, there was a loud noise, "like a mighty wind." If you were in the middle of a church service today and heard such a sound, you might well think that a tornado was approaching. To these are added "tongues, as of fire." Again, if you were in church and saw such a sight, you would probably run for the door and the telephone to call 911!

Why are these details important? Because we are so used to reading the Book of Acts and so accustomed to speaking of the Holy Spirit that we often forget that we are speaking of a surprising, awesome, terrifying power. This event is not child's play. This is not just something to make us feel good. Here we are dealing with the very power that holds the universe and the atoms together.

8

The Acts of the Spirit

The book you have begun to study has justly been called the "Acts of the Spirit." If so, you must enter it with a sense of expectation that you will find wondrous things. You may well discover a power and a joy heretofore unknown to us. You should also enter this book with a sense of trepidation that you may also have to face up to some fairly radical demands on your lives and the life of the church!

Keep on reading. Ancient people began to speak in a number of different languages. It must have been quite confusing. It was Babel all over again! Can you imagine how you would feel if, when your class meets to study this passage, one person would start speaking French, another Swahili, another Tamil, another Aymara, and so on?

What Was the Purpose?

Was there a purpose to all of these languages being spoken? Various people living in Jerusalem were all Jews who shared a common heritage. They had grown up in different parts of the world, and therefore they had different native languages. Thanks to the confusing multitude of languages that the disciples spoke, bystanders were able to hear "each of us, in our own native language." Jesus had told his disciples that they would receive the Spirit so that they could be witnesses. Not surprisingly, when one considers our unique vantage point in history, that was precisely what happened!

"But," you may say, "these people could all understand either Greek or Aramaic. Somehow they were able to communicate with each other. Why, then, would they need to hear in all these different languages?"

That is precisely the point. What is needed is more than merely being able to understand. *What is needed is being able to appropriate the Christian message into one's own context or culture.* There were common languages that people could use to understand each other, largely languages of trade and empire—languages that one learned out of necessity, not the languages of the cradle, the languages in which various people would express their innermost feelings. They were not the languages the Spirit used. The Spirit used the language of each so that each could hear and be obedient in each one's particular culture and context.

In a way, that is what the global mission of the church has been through the centuries: to speak the message by the power of the Spirit in each particular language and culture of the world. This idea has more direct implications for us. Very often when we think of inviting people to join the church, we think of inviting them to become like us. There is a certain sense in which that is necessary. We invite others to become Christians, just as we are Christians. Do we also expect them to behave exactly as we do? to dress as we dress? to speak as we speak? to join the church on our terms?

9

How Will We Respond to the Challenges?

As we study the Book of Acts, we shall repeatedly see that what the Spirit does is allow the church to speak to various people on their own terms, within their own situations. We shall see that this was a difficult lesson for the church to learn. Indeed, it was a lesson that the church had to learn again and again—and still may have to learn.

Dimension 4:
A Daily Bible Journey Plan

Day 1: Acts 1:1-5

Day 2: Acts 1:6-11

Day 3: Acts 1:12-26

Day 4: Acts 2:1-13

Day 5: Acts 2:14-36

Day 6: Acts 2:37-42

Day 7: Acts 2:43-47

*A*UTHORITY

What to Watch For

As you read the passage for this study, be on the lookout for issues of power and prestige. You will come across several characters, some of them famous, and some of them not. Ask the same questions about each of them (or at least about each group of them):

➤ At the time of the events, what social prestige or standing did this person have?
➤ What was the basis of that standing?
➤ Who, if anyone, in the story threatens that standing or might be thought to do so?

While remaining as closely tied as possible to the biblical text, try to discover (or at least to imagine) the possible motivations that various people might have had for their actions. Watch for the emotions and attitudes that the text expresses or implies. (For instance, look for annoyance, boldness, puzzlement, or praise.)

If you wish to read the continuation of this story, read also Acts 5:12-42.

A good way to approach this text is to outline the movement of the scene from place to place. Thus:

1. Where were Peter and John speaking?

2. Where were they taken? Why?

3. Where were they taken the next day? (Even though the exact place is not mentioned, the scene is described.)

A Central Theme in the Nation of Israel

In order to understand the passage we are studying, it is necessary to review a process that begins in chapter 3 and includes most of chapters 4 and 5.

In chapter 3, we are told that, as Peter and John were entering the Temple at the hour of prayer, a beggar who could not walk asked them for alms. Instead, Peter told him, "I have no silver or gold, but what I have I give you; in the name of Jesus Christ of Nazareth, stand up and walk" (6). Peter then took him by the hand and raised him. The man not only walked but also started leaping and followed Peter and John into the Temple. When people who had known the lame man for years saw this, they were amazed. Eventually, in the place called Solomon's Portico, Peter addressed the people with a sermon quoted extensively in Acts.

In chapter 4, we are told that Peter and John were still addressing "the people" when something happened. Before we move further in the story, it is important to underline this term, *the people*. *The people* is a term with theological significance, for throughout the Old Testament, and as a central theme in the religion of Israel, we hear of "the people of God," or "the people of the covenant." Thus, "the people" did not mean just a conglomerate of individuals. It was Israel itself, the covenant people whom God had brought through the Red Sea.

12

	ELITE	PEOPLE
4:1	priests; captain of the temple, Sadducees	speaking to the people
4:2		teaching the people
4:5-6	rulers; elders; scribes; Annas the high priest; Caiaphas; John; Alexander; and all who were of the priestly family	
4:8	rulers of the people and elders	
4:10	to all of you	to all the people of Israel
4:17		from spreading further among the people
4:21	finding no way to punish them	because of the people

Keeping this contrast in mind, look at the story as Luke tells it.

In this case, however, there was a further dimension to "the people." As you continue reading the text, note the contrast between "the people" and "the elite." The preceding chart may help you see that contrast.

A Study in Contrasts

Peter and John were speaking to *the people* when *the priests, the captain of the temple,* and *the Sadducees* entered the picture. Although not all priests were part of the elite, in this context it is clear that Luke was referring to those who were serving in the Temple and who would be related or connected with the high priest and his family. The "captain of the temple" (or, in a more literal translation, the "general" of the Temple), was the head of a special guard composed entirely of Levites. The Sadducees as such did not hold a specific office. Generally this was the party of the higher classes, those more willing to collaborate with Rome because they benefitted from trade and the status quo. In other words, what we have here is a combination of the *official* holders of power with the *extraofficial* authorities, who are no less powerful even though they hold no particular office.

All of these appeared on the scene. They were *annoyed* for two reasons. First, they were annoyed because the apostles were *teaching the people*. This first reason for annoyance was a matter of authority. Persons such as these had no right to teach the people. If they insisted on teaching, that very act undermined established authorities and procedures. The second reason for their annoyance was theological: they were *proclaiming that in Jesus there was resurrection of the dead*. One of the doctrinal positions that characterized the Sadducees was that they denied resurrection. The apostles' preaching, besides being unauthorized, contradicted the influential Sadducees. Therefore, all these various people in power, annoyed at what the apostles were doing, put them in prison.

A Challenge to Authority

The trial was to be held the next day. Again, those who sat in judgment were the "rulers, elders, and scribes." Luke mentioned several in particular: "Annas the high priest, Caiaphas, John, and Alexander, and all who were of the high-priestly family" (6).

The question, which was posed before the accused, made it clear that what was at stake was the fear that these Galileans might have been trying to usurp the authority of the powerful. "By what power or by what name did you do this?" (7) They were not concerned about the action itself of healing the lame man. What worried them was the possible challenge to authority.

Peter's reply showed that he understood. He addressed those before him as "rulers of the people and elders" (8). He clarified that they were being "questioned today because of a good deed done to someone who was sick" (9). In other words, Peter and John were, in fact, accused of doing good without proper authorization. Finally, before launching into the body of his speech, Peter noted that there were in fact two different sorts of possible audiences: "let it be known to all of you [that is, to the rulers and elders], and to all the *people* of Israel" (10).

The rest of the speech focused on the same issue leading to the quote from Psalm 118:

> "the stone that was rejected by you, the builders;
> it has become the cornerstone."

In other words, the leaders of Israel, who were supposed to be building up the people of God, rejected the one who was to be the most important stone of the entire building.

A Matter of Healing and Salvation

Verse 12 is the most often quoted verse in Peter's speech. "There is salvation in no one else, for there is no other name . . . by which we must be saved." You might ask, "Why did Peter suddenly start speaking about salvation when he was questioned about a miracle of healing?" The answer, at least in part, is that in Greek (the language in which Acts was written) there is a single word for what we understand by "healing" and by "saving." Thus, the miracle about which Peter and John were being questioned was a matter of healing/saving (that is, the word that verse 9 translates as "has been healed"). They were being asked by what power or name they had done this healing/salvation? Peter's speech ended with a clear answer to the question posed. The only name in which there was any healing/salvation was the name of Jesus Christ of Nazareth.

The response of the Council once again showed the degree to which questions of social standing were at stake. The Council saw the boldness of Peter and John. The Council also saw that they were "uneducated and ordinary men." They "were amazed and recognized them as companions of Jesus" (13). What was meant by this expression was that they saw in them what they had seen in Jesus—the boldness to stand up against those seemingly much more powerful than themselves and to confront them in the name of God. The Council also saw the man who had been healed, who many knew had been lame for over forty years (22). Therefore, they could not simply deny that anything had happened. Caught in that situation, the leaders of the Council followed the typical procedure of the powerful.

A Bit of Damage Control

First of all the Council leaders called for a closed meeting, where they discussed their situation and analyzed possible options for keeping their prestige intact. Once they decided that they could not deny what was common knowledge—that the man had been healed—they proceeded to control the damage. Their goal was "to keep it from spreading further among the people" (17). (Note again that the elite had constituted itself guardian of what the people should and should not know.)

The apostles were ordered "not to speak or teach at all in the name of Jesus" (18). What did this entail? It meant that neither Peter nor John could teach or speak about Jesus. They could not claim the authority of Jesus in order to teach or speak.

When Peter and John replied that they could not obey such an order since it would mean disobeying God, one might have expected that the Council would have reacted forcefully or even violently. However, the Council itself faced a quandary. Those who comprised the Council did not dare punish Jesus' disciples, because *the people* had all seen that the lame man was healed. Furthermore, we are told in verse 22 that the man, who was lame from birth, was over forty years old, thus adding to the wonder of his being healed. Therefore, all the Council dared to do was to threaten the disciples once more and let them go.

Issues of Power and Prestige

Verse 12 is so impressive, that sometimes Bible students pay little attention to the rest of the passage. Even less do students of the Bible pay attention to the issues of power and prestige that are so central to the passage.

Taking these matters into account, note that the text deals with issues
that have remained relevant. Bible students could certainly analyze the
way politics is conducted both in our nation and throughout the world and
see there the same issues of power and prestige that were at play in the
story in Acts. The attempt to silence the apostles is quite reminiscent of
what politicians today call "damage control"!

Politics and Power Hamper Our Mission

It is not only in government and politics that we see these issues at work.
We can see them also in the church. Sometimes they seriously hamper the
mission of the church.

There are several countries throughout the world where people in power
seek to curtail the church's witness. In some cases there are military dicta-
torships who fear that the work of the church may create unrest. In other
cases there are leaders of various religions who fear that Christianity will
compete with that religion for the allegiance of the people. In still other
cases there are rich landholders who accuse Christian leaders of organiz-
ing peasants to claim the land. In all these cases, we must remember that
we are all one church, and we must remember all of these sisters and
brothers in our prayers, just as in the early church, when some were in
trouble, the rest of the church prayed for them (Acts 12:5).

While we are fortunate that in the United States we do not see the
extreme and violent opposition that we see in other places, we must not
assume naively that similar opposition does not exist. Quite often, when
the church tries to perform its mission in a particular community, there are
those who oppose it because they see their interests threatened. Think, for
instance, of cases in which someone opposes a shelter for the homeless, or
a food kitchen, or a sports program for poor children. Do you see any connection between such opposition and the attitude of the Jewish leaders
before Peter and John?

Our Power and Prestige May Be Threatened

On the other hand, when we read this text in Acts we must not be too
quick to identify ourselves with the apostles. Sometimes, quite often in

Some of these Jews were considered "more Jewish" than the others. These were the ones who had generally grown up in Palestine or nearby. To distinguish them from the others, they were called "Hebrews." This was because, in the common language of the time, Aramaic was often called "Hebrew." Since these Jews spoke Aramaic (nobody spoke real Hebrew anymore as a daily language), they were called "Hebrews."

The Hellenists Lived Among Gentiles

The "others" were often called Hellenists. They were not Greeks. They too were Jews. The Hellenists had merely grown up in a different setting. They had grown up or spent most of their lives away from Palestine, usually in various areas of what was by then the Roman Empire. They probably spoke many languages, according to the land where they had been raised. Since Greek was the common language of trade and culture in the entire eastern Mediterranean, they usually spoke Greek, and often used that language to talk among themselves. Therefore, they were called "Hellenists."

If you recall how frequently in the Old Testament Israel was punished for its lack of fidelity to God, you will understand how many among the Hebrews looked at the Hellenists—not just in the church but in Jewish society at large—as being not as good as the rest of the Jews. Living among Gentiles as they did, they could not keep themselves pure and undefiled. Perhaps the difficult times through which Israel was going was due to the presence of these Hellenists!

The Hellenist Widows

To make matters worse, there were in Jerusalem a disproportionately high number of needy Hellenist widows. Many of these Hellenists still retained a high regard for Jerusalem and the Holy Land. Therefore, as they aged, many would go there to spend their last years. In many cases, this left widows spending their last years in Jerusalem, waiting till they could join their husbands in the grave. This rankled the Hebrews, who resented the growing number of needy people to whom they must contribute support.

Other translations say that there was "murmuring." In any case, this was not a formal complaint, but the sort of shapeless discontent that will normally arise in such situations.

The Book of Acts tells us that this situation began to impinge on the life of the church. Eventually, there was a complaint, that the Hellenist widows were not receiving their just share in the distribution of resources.

The Election of the Seven

In a way, although perhaps not explicitly, the complaint was directed against the Twelve, for Acts has already told us that they were the ones who would receive what was to be distributed among the needy (4:35). You might expect them to react otherwise. What they did was suggest that seven men be selected by the whole community. Henceforth, there was a sort of division of labor, with the Twelve continuing to devote themselves to prayer and to preaching, and the seven others being in charge of the management of the church's resources to serve the needy.

The laying on of hands was an ancient ceremony that could indicate consecration (as in the case of an animal to be sacrificed), blessing (as a father blessing a son), or passing on of authority (as a king naming an heir). In this particular case, it probably was intended to signify a combination of the last two. However, knowing that Stephen would become the first Christian martyr, one is tempted to think that, in his case at least, the laying on of hands was also a sign of preparation for sacrifice.

This proposal must have been agreeable to the congregation, which elected seven men. Yet, they did do something very surprising. If their names are any indication, they elected seven Hellenists! Not one of the seven names is a typically "Hebrew" name. All were Greek names: Stephen, Philip, Prochorus, Nicanor, Timon, Parmenas, and Nicolaus. Of all these names, only Philip was sufficiently common that we can imagine a Hebrew giving it to a son—and even that would be unusual, for Philip was the name of Alexander the Great's father, and it was precisely Alexander who had brought about the enormous spread of Hellenism. Furthermore, Acts tells us that one of them, Nicolaus, was not even a Jew by birth. He was "a proselyte of Antioch" (5), which means that he had been born a Gentile and accepted Judaism and circumcision at a later date. After the congregation elected these seven men, the apostles confirmed their election by praying and laying their hands on them.

Verse 7 seems to come as an interruption in the narrative, which will pick up on Stephen (one of the seven) in verse 8. However, it has an important role here. It serves, first of all, to indicate the connection between the fact that the church dealt with issues of justice in its own midst and its continued growth. One would expect that, having given positions of such authority to a group of Hellenists, the church would have become even more suspect, and thus ceased to grow. The opposite happened.

Furthermore, Acts added that "many of the priests became obedient to the faith" (7). You may find this surprising, since up to this point most of the priests mentioned had been quite resistant to the new faith. The fact is that at that time there were in Jerusalem thousands of priests, many quite needy, who had practically no relation with the high priest and his family or with the elite they represented. This fact points to the second reason why this verse is inserted at this point. It shows that, even though the church now had a measure of Hellenistic leadership, their inclusion did not keep the Hebrews—or even the priests—away. Then comes one of the great surprises of the text.

Stephen Was One of the Seven

Stephen was one of the seven. He was supposed to be administering the resources of the church, not preaching. That was the task of the Twelve. The Scriptures indicate, however, that he had begun, if not to preach in a formal sense, at least to argue with others about the truth of Christian claims. Eventually, Stephen, who was not supposed to be preaching, preached the longest sermon in the whole Book of Acts (7:2-53)!

What this means is that, with the story of the conflict between the Hebrews and the Hellenists, we have reached one more step in the constantly developing mission of the early church. Up to this point, although Jews from various parts of the world had been added, the leadership had remained essentially the same. Now for the first time we begin hearing of a new leadership coming out of those who had come into the church most recently. Surprisingly enough, soon these new leaders were expanding the mission of the church.

In Acts 7, Stephen preached to the same group to whom Peter and John had spoken before. The difference is that the one who was speaking was a Hellenist Jewish Christian. Perhaps his being a Hellenist was the reason why, for the first time, the enemies of Christianity were able to stir up "the people as well as the elders and the scribes" (6:12).

In Acts 8, another of the seven, Philip, took center stage as he preached the gospel, first in Samaria, and then to an Ethiopian. The circle kept expanding.

WHAT'S AHEAD IN THE STORY?

➤ Acts 9 tells of the conversion of Saul, who became the main Christian figure very quickly.

➤ Acts 10 tells the story of how Peter became a missionary to the Gentile Cornelius, and in the following chapter we are told what the church in Jerusalem learned from that mission.

➤ In Acts 12 we are given the last fairly detailed report about the church in Jerusalem.

➤ From that point on, beginning with chapter 13, Acts follows the story of the Gentile mission, particularly as it developed through the ministry of Paul.

A Pivotal Point in the Story

The election of the seven was a pivotal point in the story of the early church. If at that point the Twelve had decided not to listen to the complaints of the Hellenists, or if the church in Jerusalem had decided to appoint seven Hebrews to manage its resources, who knows what would have become of the worldwide mission of the church?

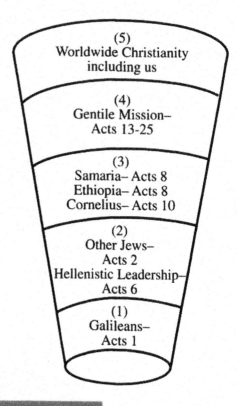

(5)
Worldwide Christianity including us

(4)
Gentile Mission–
Acts 13-25

(3)
Samaria– Acts 8
Ethiopia– Acts 8
Cornelius– Acts 10

(2)
Other Jews–
Acts 2
Hellenistic Leadership–
Acts 6

(1)
Galileans–
Acts 1

Dimension 3:
What Does the Bible Mean to Us?

Whose Shoes Are We In?

As we seek to apply this text to our situation, perhaps the first thing we ought to consider is whether to place ourselves in the shoes of the Hebrews or of the Hellenists.

In order to do this, we might say that the Hebrews were the ones who traditionally held the authority and who were being challenged by the Hellenists. The latter were those who, either because they were relatively recent arrivals or for some other reason, were usually not given access to the places where decisions were made. This includes even decisions that seriously affected their lives, as in the case of the distribution of support to the Hellenist widows.

Probably, for most of us, there are situations in which we belong to one category, and other situations in which we belong to another. Let us consider some examples:

➤ If you are a white, middle-class, and native English-speaking person, there are many situations where you are more like the Hebrews. For example, perhaps you are in a denomination in which traditionally power has been held by people like you. Now there are a number of people of different backgrounds joining the denomination; they ask for the space to make the decisions that most closely affect their lives. If that is the case, you are a "Hebrew," and they are "Hellenists."

➤ If you are a woman, no matter your race or culture, there are also situations in which you are a "Hellenist" in comparison with the traditionally male-dominated structures of much of the church.

➤ If you are an ethnic minority woman, and are part of the "old guard" of your local congregation, you may well be a "Hebrew" in relation to those who are joining the church more recently, and who need space to be themselves within the Christian community.

Thus, for most of us, there are moments and relationships in which we should look at ourselves as Hebrews and other moments when we should look at ourselves as Hellenists. Having said that, what does the text tell us?

Complaints Should Be Taken Seriously

It tells us, first of all, that in those situations in which we are "Hebrews," we should take complaints or "murmuring" seriously. There are many jokes about gossip in the church. Gossip, especially when it involves a sense of unfairness, must be taken very seriously. Often that is the only way in which the "Hellenists" can make themselves heard. If the "Hebrews" ignore such rumblings, they risk ignoring the causes for friction, until the accumulated bitterness explodes.

Secondly, no matter whether you are a "Hellenist" or a "Hebrew," it is important to understand that in a situation of injustice or unfairness it is usually the people suffering the injustice who best understand it. The same is true in situations of inequality. In some ways, the people who best understand how the welfare system works—and even more, how and where it does not work—are those who must live off welfare. The early church showed its wisdom in this regard by trusting the distribution of its resources precisely to those who had most suffered the inequality in the previous system. If they were honest and fair, they would be able to do a better job, precisely because they understood the problems.

Thirdly, no matter whether you are a "Hebrew" or a "Hellenist," you must understand that the only way to deal with situations of inequality is the empowerment of those who most lack power. The "Hebrews" may act toward the "Hellenists" with gracious and even self-sacrificing charity; but as long as the "Hellenists" do not have access to the resources themselves, the relationship will be unequal. For "Hebrews," this means a readiness to relinquish power. For "Hellenists," it means two things: first, an insistence on being given a fair share of power; secondly, the commitment to use such power fairly once it is received.

This does not necessarily imply confrontation. In the case that we are studying in Acts, there seems to have been no confrontation—mainly because the Twelve were ready to hear the complaint of the Hellenists. If the "Hebrews" had refused to listen to the just claims of the "Hellenists," confrontation would, no doubt, have been inevitable.

Reflect on Your Own Congregation

Now look at your own church. Are there in your church, groups or individuals who are ignored or who receive unequal treatment? Are there groups who are underrepresented in the decision-making processes? Are there individuals who are generally ignored or bypassed? Are there "murmurings" to which we should listen?

It is very easy to answer no. That may well be the truth, and in that case you and your church are fortunate. Before you respond too quickly, however, take a moment to think. Are there persons in your congregation who are limited in their ability to leave home who are generally forgotten except for an occasional visit from the pastor? Are there young people whose ideas are consistently turned down as too impractical or unworkable? Is there a group that considers itself the "leadership" of the congregation, and from which most of the officers of the church are elected? Have you ever felt excluded or ignored? Are there others who feel the same way? If you answer yes to any of these questions, the story of the manner in which the early church dealt with the tensions between Hebrews and Hellenists could be very fruitful for you and for your entire church.

The Word of God Continued to Spread

Notice now that Acts tells us, just after the story of the election of the seven, that "the word of God continued to spread" (6:7). Luke did not insert these words capriciously. They were inserted to remind us that there is a connection between justice and mission. Do you want your church to be a growing and vital church? Then make certain that it is a community that deals with issues of inequality in its midst with the wisdom with which the early church confronted similar issues.

Day 1: Acts 6:1-7
Day 2: Acts 6:8-15
Day 3: Acts 7:1-16
Day 4: Acts 7:17-43
Day 5: Acts 7:44-53
Day 6: Acts 7:54–8:1a
Day 7: Acts 8:1b-3

Acts
8:4-25

4 *P*OWER

What to Watch For

In Acts, chapter 6, the seven were elected. In the rest of chapter 6 and in chapter 7, Stephen's speech before the Council and his death were recorded. In chapter 8 we will be told of the ministry of another of the seven, Philip. As you read, watch for the following:

➤ Note that this Philip is not the same as Philip the apostle. This Philip is one of the seven. The other was one of the Twelve.

➤ In chapter 8, there are two main stories about Philip's ministry: the one we are studying and the one about the conversion of the Ethiopian eunuch (8:26-40).

➤ The episode we are studying has to do with Simon Magus, one of Philip's converts in Samaria and what he did when he saw that people received the Holy Spirit when the apostles laid their hands on them.

➤ What is most important throughout the whole Book of Acts is not what was said about Simon Magus or about Philip but what the entire story tells us about the Holy Spirit.

1. Where did these events take place?

2. Who are the main characters in the story?

3. What do we know about Simon before his conversion?

4. Why do you think Peter reacted so negatively?

The Story of Simon Magus

As you read the text, you will see that the main story has to do with Simon Magus. Yet, there are three other portions that relate to that story and that serve as an introduction (8:4-8), as a middle link (8:14-17), and as an epilogue (8:25). You may see this best in graphic form:

Introduction (8:4-8)		Middle Link (8:14-17)		Epilogue (8:25)
	Beginning of Simon's story (8:5-13)		Conclusion of Simon's story (8:18-24)	

Christians Were Scattered

The introduction begins by telling us that, as a result of persecution in Jerusalem, many Christians were scattered. They went "from place to place, proclaiming the word" (4). One of those who was forced to leave Jerusalem was Philip, who went to Samaria preaching "the Messiah"— that is, that Jesus was the Anointed One who had been promised. There his message was well received. Many listened eagerly.

It is in the midst of that successful preaching and joyous reception that the figure of Simon was introduced. He was first presented as "a certain man named Simon [who] had previously practiced magic" (9). Although the term "previously" could be understood otherwise, what it probably meant was that he practiced magic until the time of his own conversion. At any rate, he was a very important personage in Samaria, for he "amazed the people," claiming "that he was someone great" (9). His success had been enormous, for he was praised by "all of them, from the least to the greatest" (10), and what they said was no less than, "This man is the power of God that is called great" (10). Again in verse 11 we are told that "he had amazed them with his magic" (11). We are not told that he was a particularly bad man. All that we are told is that he spoke of himself in rather grandiose terms, and that he managed to convince the crowds that all that he said about himself—and probably more—was true.

The "Amazer" Was Himself Amazed

Verses 12 and 13 tell us how far things changed with Philip's preaching. When the people of the city, all of whom had been amazed by Simon, heard Philip, they were convinced by him and were baptized. That implies that they rejected Simon's magic and Simon's claims. That was not all. Simon, too, believed and was baptized. In fact, the text says that he was "amazed." Remember that the same word had been applied twice before to the people of Samaria when they saw Simon's magic. Thus, the amazer was himself amazed. Perhaps most amazing of all, is that there is no word here of Simon opposing the preaching of Philip. In many other places in Acts we hear of people who opposed the gospel when their pocketbooks were threatened. Not so, Simon. He believed, was amazed, was baptized, and followed Philip wherever he went.

The Holy Spirit Came Upon Them

Then comes the middle link: verses 14-17. The apostles in Jerusalem heard what was happening in Samaria. They sent Peter and John—whether to inspect, to supervise, or to inspire is unclear. In any case, they arrived at the city and apparently liked what they saw, for no word of criticism was recorded there. There is only the intriguing story that the people baptized in Samaria had not received the Holy Spirit, and that when the apostles prayed for them and laid their hands on them, they received the Holy Spirit. There has been much controversy about exactly what this might mean; interpreters are far from a general consensus. What is clear—and that is the point of the story here—is that when the apostles laid their hands on these people for whom they had prayed, something extraordinary happened. There was no doubt that the Holy Spirit had come upon them.

Was Simon Magus a Hypocrite?

Returning to Simon, he saw what the apostles were doing and its result. He tried to buy this power from them, offering them money. It has been said that Simon was a hypocrite, who simply wanted to add this to his bag of tricks. The truth is that he "had previously practiced magic" (9). In other words, he had abandoned magic when he became a Christian. There is no hint in the text that any hypocrisy was involved.

Peter's answer is harsh and even devastating: "May your silver perish with you, because you thought you could obtain God's gift with money! You have no part or share in this, for your heart is not right before God. Repent therefore of this wickedness of yours, and pray to the Lord that, if possible, the intent of your heart may be forgiven you. For I see that you are in the gall of bitterness and the chains of wickedness" (20-23).

Simon was often called "Simon Magus" because he had been a magician.

This passage has been interpreted as a conflict between Simon Peter's sincerity and Simon Magus' hypocrisy. Again, the text does not shed light on sincerity or hypocrisy. What the text says is that Simon the magician, who was used to being so powerful, thought that he could exchange money (the symbol of his power in the general world of Samaria) for power and authority in the church. He was used to people speaking of him as "the power of God that is called Great" (10). Therefore, when he witnessed in Philip a power greater than his, he apparently was quite willing to submit to and follow that power. The same was true when he saw the power of the apostles, except for one thing. He apparently thought that, as a person of prestige and power in the community and one who had now become a Christian, he ought to have power in the church.

Partners in a Great Enterprise

Simon Peter, the other Simon in the story, had done nothing great on his own. He was simply a Galilean fisherman. He and James and John had been partners in the ownership of a fishing boat. They became partners in

31

a much greater enterprise. They became partners in the Spirit. As such, Simon, called Simon Peter or Simon the Rock, was a powerful man. He had come to understand the difference between the power of God and human power. Actually, some time before, precisely because he did not understand that difference and wanted to spare his Master the agony, the humiliation, and the defeat of the cross, his Master had said to him: "You are a hindrance to me; for you are not on the side of God, but of humans." Simon Peter, however, had the power to impart the Spirit. He had the power to share the "power of God that is called great" (10).

What was taking place, simply put, was that the very power and prestige of Simon Magus made it very difficult for him to understand more fully what Philip and Peter and John were preaching. He could understand power. With his power he could amaze. He was ready to be amazed at the power of others and even to submit to it in baptism.

This is the power of the Holy Spirit. The power of the Spirit is by definition a power that falls on whosoever the Spirit wills, without distinction of class, or sex, or age, or anything else. This is the Spirit who came upon the church in Acts 2, the spirit by whose power sons and daughters prophesy, young people see visions, and old people dream dreams. Even the most insignificant people of Samaria, who were formerly amazed at Simon's magic, had also become amazers. "The power of God that is called Great" (10) dwelt in them.

Could Simon Magus really accept a power to be shared by all, "from the least to the greatest," (10) who until recently were amazed at Simon himself? A power to be given equally to him and to those who until yesterday thought that he was the greatest thing on earth? A power he could not use to control others? Certainly not. This power he had to control, he had to possess, he had to buy.

Precisely because, although he could very well understand power, he could not understand nor accept this kind of power, Simon Peter told him that he had "no part or share" (21) in what was going on.

Not the End of the Story

This, however, was not the end of the story. Verse 24 seems to indicate that Simon repented, for he answered: "Pray for me to the Lord, that nothing of what you have said may happen to me."

Finally, verse 25 is an epilogue to the entire story. Peter and John, who had come to the city to see the results of Philip's work there, returned to Jerusalem, and on the way proclaimed "the good news to many villages of the Samaritans" (25). The epilogue is important in the scheme and purpose of Acts. One of Luke's concerns in writing the Book of Acts was those who felt that the mission to the Gentiles was ill-conceived. Luke was slowly moving his readers from mission in Judea to a wider vision and using the mission to Samaria as a bridge before he moved to the rest of the world. In sharing that Peter and John stopped to preach in the villages of the Samaritans, he was informing readers, who had questions on the validity of the Gentile mission, that at least on the mission to the Samaritans the apostles concurred. Later on, he said the same about the mission to the Gentiles.

Dimension 3: What Does the Bible Mean to Us?

Simon Was a Sincere Believer

In many sermons and commentaries, we hear or read that Simon was a worthless hypocrite. Let us give Simon the benefit of the doubt, however, reading only what is in the text. The emerging image of Simon is very different from that which we have received in popular tradition. Simon was a sincere believer. He may not have known too well what it was that he had believed in; but that could hardly be held against him, seeing that the disciples themselves were more than a little befuddled by the teachings of Jesus. Apparently he was a sincere believer.

He was also a powerful man. According to the text, his power and prestige were such that all paid heed to him, from the least to the greatest. The people around him said: "This man is the power of God that is called Great" (10). Today we would say that he was "a pillar in the community."

Having said all this, it seems clear that a valid way to look at this text, rather than from the point of view of sincerity and hypocrisy (of which the text makes no mention) is from the point of view of power and its workings, which the text does emphasize. Again, they all, from the least to the greatest, said of Simon: "This man is the power of God that is called Great" (10). The matter of amazement, which the text refers both to Simon's magic and to the signs accompanying Philip's preaching, was certainly an issue of response to perceived power.

The Text Refers to Us

Time has gone by, and we have found ways to avoid dealing with the harsh lessons of this text. One way is by mystifying it. It deals with magicians, and signs, and miracles. Therefore, it must belong to an alien world and have nothing to do with us.

A second way is by theologizing it. I suspect that much of what we call "theology" is simply a means to avoid having to deal with issues of obedience. We could spend forever—indeed, churches have spent forever—debating the laying on of hands or the kind of baptism that the Samaritans had received. And, while engaged in such debates, we have to do nothing about the text and our lives today.

Or, we could avoid the radical impact of the text by psychologizing it. Simon Magus was a hypocrite, we say. No matter that the text does not say so. He must have been a hypocrite. Since we are not hypocrites—at least, not most of the time—the text does not refer to us.

Yet the text does indeed refer to us. The same dynamic of power and the cloudiness it can cause is still at work. It is at work on a personal level. It is at work at the level of churches and nations.

There are some of us who belong to traditionally powerful groups, or to traditionally powerful churches. It is from that perspective that the interpretation according to which Simon Magus was simply a hypocrite came; for, if his problem was hypocrisy, we can be certain of escaping it as long as we are sincere. But if his problem was power, the situation is much more difficult. Hernán Cortés, a *conquistadore*, was a sincere Christian; yet he decimated populations of native peoples. Many southern slaveholders were sincere Christians; yet they participated in human slavery. Sincerity is not enough, especially when sincerity is blinded with power.

Is There Hope?

This is not to condemn the powerful. It is to point out to them that there is hope; but that this hope can only come through repentance, just as mighty Simon the Magician pleaded with Simon the fisherman: "Pray for me to the Lord" (24).

This is our only option. We must recognize that the power of the Spirit is different from the power of Simon Magus, different from the power of money, and different from the power of prestige. This is the Simon Peter option. It is an option that is both open to share its power ("the apostles laid their hands on them, and they received the Holy Spirit") and firm as to the nature of that power ("your silver perish with you, because you thought you could obtain God's gift with money! You have no part or share in this matter, for your heart is not right before God"). It does not seek power for itself, but seeks and receives power in order to share it.

Thanks be to God, the hope of Simon Peter is still ours today. Do we wish to be powerful in evangelism? Let us begin by recognizing that it is not a matter of how well we plan our evangelistic outreach, nor even of how much money we put into it, but that true evangelism, like the rest of the life of the church, only takes place by the power of the Holy Spirit.

Do we wish to speak a powerful word to our society? Let us begin by challenging whatever dehumanizing structures of power there may be not only in society but also in the church.

Do we really wish to be faithful in our stewardship? Let us begin by telling those who think that their money buys them some special privilege in the church ("your silver perish with you").

It may sound terrible. Some of us won't like it at all. After all, we may have more money, more education, better health than the vast majority of humankind. We may have already lived much longer than the life expectancy of most people in the world. In many ways, we are privileged. Therefore, we do not like the implications of this passage.

Pray for Me to the Lord

Simon Magus, whom tradition has used as a theological and moral whipping boy, shows us all the way to a new hope: "Pray for me to the Lord." There is no other way than the way of repentance. There is no other way for us today, enmeshed as we are in the sin of Simon, than to say to each other: "Pray for me to the Lord."

Dimension 4:
A Daily Bible Journey Plan

Day 1: Acts 8:4-25

Day 2: Acts 8:26-40

Day 3: Acts 9:1-9

Day 4: Acts 9:10-19a

Day 5: Acts 9:19b-25

Day 6: Acts 9:26-31

Day 7: Acts 9:32-43

5 CONVERSION

What to Watch For

The Book of Acts has many turning points—places where the unexpected happens and the story takes off in a new direction. We have already seen some of these places: Pentecost, the development of a Hellenistic leadership, or the beginning of persecution.

Now we arrive at another such turning point, the conversion of Paul. This chapter is so pivotal in the entire Book of Acts that one can imagine it as a hinge dividing the book in two parts. From now on, Paul will occupy an increasingly important role in the story.

➤ In chapters 10-12 we shall return to Peter and to Jerusalem.
➤ By chapter 13 we shall be fully into the Gentile mission of which Paul was the outstanding leader.
➤ At first, Paul shared the limelight with Barnabas; but eventually he became the center of attention.

The passage we are studying today tells us how the relentless persecutor of Christianity became one of its adherents and hints at the great things that God would do through him.

1. In your readings of the earlier sections of Acts, where have you already encountered Saul?

2. Even apart from what you know of Saul's later life, and based only on today's text, what changes can you see in him?

3. What changes can you see in Ananias?

On the Road to Damascus

The story is well known—so well known that often we miss its drama. Try to read it as if it were the very first time, and you did not know the end.

Saul, the one who had been persecuting the church by entering house after house and dragging off men and women (Acts 8:3), planned to widen the scope of persecution. He had gone to the high priest and asked for letters of introduction to take to the synagogues at Damascus. Here he intended to get help in finding any followers of Jesus who may have taken refuge in that city so that he could bring them back to Jerusalem in chains.

The distance between Jerusalem and Damascus was some 150 miles and must have taken several days. Just as he was about to reach the end of his journey, a light flashed around him and he fell to the ground. Then he heard a voice.

The following dialogue resulted:

—"Saul, Saul, why do you persecute me?" (4)

You may also be aware that there are two other accounts of Paul's conversion in Acts, both of which Luke places on Paul's lips. These accounts are given in Acts 22:6-16 and 26:12-18. In this review of the story, we shall refer only to the account in Acts 9. You may wish to look also at the other two.

37

—"Who are you, Lord?" (5)

—"I am Jesus, whom you are persecuting. But get up and enter the city, and you will be told what you are to do" (5-6)

When he got up from the ground (we are not told how much time later), he could not see and had to be led by the hand. Notice the irony in the story. He, who had left for Damascus in high hopes and bearing letters from the high priest, entered the city blind and led by the hand!

A Street Called "Straight"

In this condition he remained for three days, eating and drinking nothing. (According to the manner in which days were counted, this could have been the rest of the day on which he had his shattering experience, one whole day, and part of the following.)

Luke changed the scene, taking us to a new place and introducing a new character whose name was Ananias.

This character should not be confused with the Ananias who was married to Sapphira, and whose death is told in chapter 5, or with Ananias, the high priest who became Paul's enemy.

Ananias had a vision, which Luke again presented in the form of a dialogue:

—"Ananias!" (10);

—"Here I am, Lord" (10);

—"Get up and go to the street called Straight, and at the house of Judas look for a man of Tarsus named Saul. At this moment he is praying, and he has seen in a vision a man named Ananias come in and lay his hands on him so that he might regain his sight" (11-12);

—"Lord, I have heard from many about this man, how much evil he has done to your saints in Jerusalem; and here he has authority from the chief priests to bind all who invoke your name" (13-14);

—"Go, for he is an instrument whom I have chosen to bring my name before Gentiles and kings and before the people of Israel; I myself will show him how much he must suffer for the sake of my name" (15-16).

The Lord's insistence overcame Ananias' resistance. He did as he had been told. He visited Saul at the house of Judas on Straight street and told Saul that he had been sent by the Lord.

The result was immediate! First, "something like scales" fell off Paul's eyes so that he could see again. Then he got up and was baptized. Finally, he started eating again and regained his strength.

Acts indicates that Saul remained with the disciples in Damascus "for several days" (19). This phrase is vague, but in this usage it could well mean that Paul stayed for several weeks or even months. During that time, apparently from the very moment of his conversion, Saul proclaimed Jesus in the synagogues. Remember that these were the same synagogues for which he had obtained letters from the high priests. That is why those who heard him were so amazed, remembering that he used to persecute Christians, and that he had come to Damascus for that sole purpose.

Luke did not tell us how it was that Saul was able to preach of Jesus, without being himself arrested and sent in chains to Jerusalem, as he had intended to do with any Christians he could find in Damascus. The answer could be that, since it was Saul who had taken the lead in the persecution, and particularly in this attempt to expand its reach, no one saw to it to get the necessary letters from the high priests to arrest Paul.

You may wish to take note that what Paul did in Damascus was similar to what he later did whenever he arrived at a new city. He preached in the synagogue. Throughout the Book of Acts, and even after he decided that his mission was primarily to the Gentiles, Paul used the synagogue as his point of entry into a new city. In places where there was no synagogue, such as Philippi, he began by looking for one.

Note the order. Once his conversion had taken place, Saul apparently was so eager to be baptized that Luke told us that Paul was baptized before he even ate! It is possible, of course, that Paul was expected to fast before baptism; this was indeed the practice in the early second century.

Luke did tell us that "Saul became increasingly more powerful" (22). Obviously, this does not mean that he became physically stronger, or that he had greater influence. It means rather that he became more powerful as a witness and a debater. He "became increasingly more powerful and confounded the Jews who lived in Damascus" (22). It was not a matter of power, such as Simon Magus had, but of power such as the Holy Spirit is able to give.

Plotters Scheme Against Paul

According to Acts, Paul's message was "that Jesus was the Son of God" (20). At this stage, this was a matter under debate. The debate was not concerned with whether Jesus was a good man or not, nor even whether he was justly or unjustly condemned to death, but rather whether he was the awaited Messiah. Paul's view—and the view of all early Christians—was that indeed Jesus was the Messiah. This was the "good news"! The Messiah had come; ancient promises were being fulfilled; the reign of God was at hand.

"Some time had passed" (23). Obviously, this lapse of time refers to the same lapse of time as the "several days" of verse 19. By then, apparently because they could not defeat him in argument, "the Jews" plotted to kill Saul. At this point, Acts used the term "the Jews," to refer only to those who did not believe in Jesus. It is not an ethnic term, for from the ethnic point of view all Christians were also Jews. Thus, the non-Christian Jews

39

plotted to kill Saul, presumably because he was converting too many of them, or simply because they could not defeat him in argument.

With a touch of drama, and yet in very few words, Luke told of what could, by itself, be the plot of an entire novel. The Jews plotted against Saul. Saul learned of it. Apparently the plotters knew that he was aware of their plan, for they set someone to watch constantly over the gates of the city so that he could not escape. Saul's disciples aided his escape by lowering him in a basket from an opening in the wall.

> Note that Luke used the term *his disciples*. In other words, Paul had remained in Damascus long enough, and his witnessing and teaching were effective enough, that he had disciples.

According to Acts, Saul then went to Jerusalem, and there again the disciples reacted in a manner similar to Ananias when he heard that he should go visit Paul. "They were all afraid of him, for they did not believe that he was a disciple" (26). Although the text did not explicitly say so, it would seem that, even though they heard that he claimed to have been converted, he might have been a pretender in order to gain admittance into the church and then unleash his persecution. In other words, they feared that he might have "gone under cover."

> Remember, speaking boldly was among the things that the Council had ordered Peter and John not to do.

At this point, it was Barnabas who intervened. Barnabas believed Paul's testimony. He introduced him to the apostles. When Saul told them of his experience, he was accepted as one of the group of followers of Jesus, and began "speaking boldly in the name of the Lord" (28).

Here again the outcome was similar to what happened in Damascus and what would happen in most places where Paul went. He began arguing with "the Hellenists"—apparently the same sort of Hellenistic Jew who had taken the lead in accusing Stephen before the Council. Their reaction was the same as in Stephen's case. "They were attempting to kill him" (29).

Once again, other believers learned of the Hellenists' plans and did what other disciples had done in Damascus. They helped Saul escape. They took him to Caesarea, the port serving Jerusalem; from there they traveled to Tarsus, a city sufficiently far away that Paul's enemies would have no influence there. Not coincidentally, Tarsus was also Paul's home.

Dimension 3:
What Does the Bible Mean to Us?

The Proud Persecutor Is Himself Persecuted

This is an all-time favorite among Bible passages. Probably it owes part of its popularity to the intense drama of the story. The one who set out from

Jerusalem a proud persecutor of the disciples entered Damascus a humbled, blind, dependent, willing disciple himself. To add to the drama, we read this story in the light of what we know would happen later. The former persecutor of Christianity would become its foremost preacher and apostle.

There is probably another, deeper reason for the popularity of this passage: it responds to an inner need all of us feel. It tells us that, no matter who we have been or what we may have done, there is always the possibility of change, of forgiveness, of becoming a new person.

Prisoners to the Past

In the natural order of things, we are all prisoners of our past. If there is anything in our lives we cannot change, it is the past. If in the past we did something we now wish we had not done, there is no way we can change that. We may wish it had not happened the way it did. We may wish we had acted differently. We may try to change the consequences of the past by some new actions. All that may be good and even necessary; it does not undo the past. The past is still there, unerasable and inescapable. All *we* can do about it is to try either to forget it or somehow to make amends for our past actions. To leave it behind, really and absolutely, *that* we cannot do.

Paul's experience on the road to Damascus and what happened thereafter, tells us otherwise. He stood by, at least as a passive spectator, and probably as an active instigator, when Stephen was stoned. He persecuted the church. Luke did not give us details of that persecution. It is clear, however, that it was severe enough that many believers had to leave Jerusalem because of it. He had been zealous enough in that persecution to take the initiative to expand it to distant Damascus.

Obviously, Paul did all these things believing he was serving God. There is no hint, however, either in this story or elsewhere in the entire New Testament that this belief made his actions less evil.

On the road to Damascus he had an experience that showed him that he was terribly wrong in what he was doing and what he had done. As a consequence of that experience, he ceased persecuting Christians, and joined those whom he had previously hated and persecuted.

Yet that is not the most surprising element in the story. *What is most surprising is that Paul was never told that he was to earn forgiveness for all the evil he had done.* He was not told: "Because you did all this evil, now you must devote your life to doing good so that you can clear your balance sheet." He was simply offered a new way of life. That new life began with forgiveness—free, absolutely free forgiveness.

41

The Past Can Be Left Behind

That is the good news of the gospel for us: the past can *really, completely, absolutely,* be left behind. We can start anew—not because of something we do, but because that is what God's grace does for us. Paul himself put it quite forcefully when he wrote to the Corinthians: "If anyone is in Christ, there is a new creation: everything old has passed away; see, everything has become new!" (2 Corinthians 5:17).

The very first thing we must hear as we listen to the story of Paul's conversion is that the same is true for each one of us. The slate can be totally erased. Furthermore, we can even begin with a new slate! That is the good news of the gospel.

That is why we dare approach God when we pray—God, whom we have so grievously wronged in so many ways! That is why we can live joyously in spite of our many sins and shortcomings. The Lord who called and forgave Saul still calls and forgives today!

We must also remember, however, that what we have received we must also be ready to have others receive. Unfortunately, Christians have often been quite ready to claim forgiveness for themselves, but deny it to others. This very morning, before writing these words, I heard a preacher over the radio tell how his sins had been forgiven, and what a terrible sinner he had been until he came to Jesus. Not two minutes after this moving testimony he was lambasting everyone who did not agree with him in every detail of doctrine, questioning the sincerity of women who come to church with showy jewelry and attacking another church across town that had begun a ministry among people infected with AIDS.

Probably most of us do not go to that extreme. However, it is still quite plausible that some will act as if they had somehow earned the forgiveness and the new life that we enjoy through Christ's mercy. True Christian discipleship requires, however, not only that we accept God's forgiveness, but also that we extend forgiveness to others.

Two Unnoticed Characters

There are two characters in today's Bible text who often go unnoticed, but who have much to teach us: Ananias and Barnabas.

We don't know much about Ananias. What we do know makes a point quite clearly. Here was a Christian—therefore presumably someone whose sins had been forgiven—called by God to visit someone whom he had good reason to fear. His reluctance is quite understandable. Yet, he went to Saul. And, what are his first words? *"Brother* Saul . . ." (17)!

We know a little more about Barnabas. We know that Barnabas was not his real name but one that the apostles had given him. It meant "son of encouragement" (Acts 4:36). He was the one who, when apparently not even the apostles were willing to trust Saul, trusted him. He brought Saul to the apostles (or, more precisely, trusted the Lord of forgiveness and newness of life and therefore believed that Saul could indeed change).

For Ananias or for Barnabas to have refused to accept the possibility that the Lord could recreate Saul would have shown a lack of faith, not just in Saul, but also and above all in the Lord. Likewise, when we refuse to forgive, or to believe that those whom we have known as sinners can be created anew, it is not just them that we reject. We also reject the very Lord who has forgiven us!

Dimension 4:
A Daily Bible Journey Plan

Day 1: Acts 10:1-16

Day 2: Acts 10:17-33

Day 3: Acts 10:34-48

Day 4: Acts 11:1-18

Day 5: Acts 11:19-26

Day 6: Acts 11:27-30

Day 7: Acts 12:1-5

Acts 11:19-30; 13:1-3

HORIZONS

6

What to Watch For

In our study of Acts, our horizons have been constantly expanding. If you have been reading, not only the materials for the studies themselves, but also the texts assigned for Dimension 4: A Daily Bible Journey, you will have seen this expansion quite clearly.

➤ At first, the story was limited to Jerusalem. We are told of Pentecost and of the life of the church there. Increasingly, still in Jerusalem, we see the Hellenists playing a role in the leadership of the church.
➤ The mission expanded further. Philip traveled to Samaria. He was moved by the Spirit to go meet the Ethiopian eunuch whom he baptized.
➤ Peter traveled through Judea and eventually baptized a Roman centurion and other Gentiles in Caesarea.
➤ He returned to report to Jerusalem where the church joyfully exclaimed: "Then God has given even to the Gentiles the repentance that leads to life" (Acts 11:18).

As you read and study today's passages, look both for new departures and for elements of continuity with the earlier chapters of Acts.

1. How did Christianity arrive at Antioch?

2. Who were the leaders of the church in Antioch? Where were they from?

3. What were some of the new developments that took place in Antioch?

Antioch—Home Base for Paul and Barnabas

The church in Antioch was the home base for the mission of Paul and Barnabas, which will become the focus of Acts. Note, however, that Acts makes it very clear that the notion of a mission to the Gentiles was not the invention of some innovators in Antioch. Remember also that, at the beginning of this study, we said that one of the audiences that Luke kept in mind as he wrote this book was the remnant of a Jewish Christian church. Some of its members thought that Christianity should have remained a Jewish sect and never ventured into the Gentile world.

Luke countered that notion by showing that the mission to the Gentiles was initiated, not by individuals or churches, *but by the movement of the Holy Spirit*, and that this happened in various places almost simultaneously. Let us look at this more closely.

Note that the phrase in Acts 11:19, which opens the story of the church in Antioch, is almost exactly parallel to Acts 8:4, which introduces Philip's ministry in Samaria and to the Ethiopian. The intent was to show that these events were chronologically parallel. The persecution brought about a scattering of the disciples. Philip went to Samaria, and eventually to the Ethiopian. Others went "as far as Phoenicia, Cyprus, and Antioch" (19). This was the beginning of the story we are about to read. In between, Luke tells us of a third beginning of the Gentile mission. Peter witnessed to Cornelius and his friends in Caesarea.

Thus, what Luke told about the church in Antioch and its mission is but one strand of a larger story, all woven together by the guidance of the Holy Spirit.

PHILIP'S MINISTRY

8:4: Those who were scattered

8:4-25: Philip in Samaria

8:26-40: Philip and the Ethiopian

PETER, CORNELIUS, AND THE MEN RETURN TO JERUSALEM

9:32 Peter went here and there

9:32-43 Peter in Judea among the Jews

10:1-48 Peter and Cornelius

THE BEGINNINGS AT ANTIOCH

11:19 Those who were scattered

11:19-27 Preaching to the Gentiles in Antioch

13:1-3 Saul and Barnabas sent in mission under the direction of the Holy Spirit

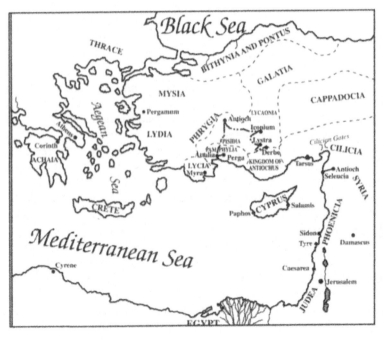

Adapted from *Bible Teacher Kit*, © 1994, by Abingdon Press

How Did Christianity Come to Antioch?

Keeping that in mind, we may look in more detail at the passage itself, which tells us of the beginnings of the church in Antioch, and how it came to take such a position of leadership in the Christian mission.

The exact way in which Christianity came to Antioch is not altogether clear. In verse 19 we are told that people scattered out of Jerusalem into areas such as Phoenicia, Cyprus, and Antioch. Verse 20 adds that some who came to Antioch were "men of Cyprus and Cyrene." Since Cyrene was far away in the opposite direction (see map inset) this second piece of information probably means, not that they came to Antioch from Jerusalem by way of Cyrene, but that among those who came from Jerusalem were some who were originally from Cyrene. The case of the "men from Cyprus" is not quite as clear, for there was ample maritime commerce between Caesarea in Judea and Cyprus as well as between Cyprus and Antioch. In any case, the important point is that Christianity arrived at Antioch, mostly because of the persecution in Jerusalem, and that the people gathered in the church there had a variety of experiences and backgrounds. At first those who came to Antioch "spoke the word to no one except Jews" (19). Later, especially after these people from Cyprus and Cyrene arrived, they "spoke to the Hellenists also" (20).

> We shall return to look at those who originated in Cyrene but had gone on to live in Jerusalem when we look at the beginning of chapter 13.

The word *Hellenists* may be confusing. When we studied Acts 6, we said that the Hellenists there were not Gentiles, but Jews of a more cosmopolitan background than the Hebrews. Here, however, the reference is to Gentiles—otherwise the contraposition between "to no one except Jews" (19) and "to the Hellenists also" (20) would make no sense. Actually, there are a number of manuscripts that say *Hellenes*, that is, Greeks or Gentiles. The rest of the story shows clearly that Luke was trying to describe here a new departure, one similar to what he had already described in the stories of Philip and the Ethiopian and of Peter and Cornelius. "The hand of the Lord was with them" (21)—that is, this was no mere human innovation, but one blessed by God.

The Title *Christians* Is Taken

When the church in Jerusalem heard what was going on in Antioch, they sent Barnabas to them. The text does not say whether he was sent in order to inspect or to inspire and support. Nor does it mention a reason why Barnabas would be the obvious choice for the task. He himself was from Cyprus, and thus may have known some of the leaders of the church in Antioch—or if not, at least he would have a similar background.

Note again the stress on the Spirit's support for the entire enterprise.

Whether sent to inspect or to encourage, Barnabas approved of what he saw, "for he was a good man, full of the Holy Spirit and of faith" (24). Instead of returning to Jerusalem to report, as we would have expected, Barnabas remained in Antioch. For all we know that was his base of operations from then on. In order to help him in his work in Antioch, he went to Tarsus (the capital of Cilicia) to look for Paul, who was preaching in his native territory (see Galatians 1:21). After that, he and Saul remained in Antioch for an entire year, strengthening the church there.

The verb translated as "were called" could also mean "called themselves."

It is at this point that Luke told us that "it was in Antioch that the disciples were first called 'Christians' " (26). This probably was a name originally given to them by their opponents, perhaps in mockery. It may also have been a name they gave themselves to indicate that they belonged to Christ.

At this point, Luke introduced a subject that became very important in Paul's letters and travels but which is seldom mentioned in Acts: the collection for the poor in Jerusalem. At that time the word *prophet* did not necessarily refer to one who would foretell the future. Instead it referred simply to a preacher inspired by God. In this case the "prophet" Agabus foretold the future.

Later on in your journey through the Bible, as you study Paul's Epistles, you will see that throughout his ministry Paul continued raising funds for the poor in Jerusalem.

He announced that there would be a great famine (which actually took place under the reign of Emperor Claudius). In response (it is not clear whether to the prophet's announcement or to the actual famine), the disciples in Antioch collected an offering. They sent Barnabas and Saul to Jerusalem, taking the offering with them. Of this visit to Jerusalem we know very little. Luke glossed over the event, apparently taking for granted that the reader would fill in the missing details. To this time, scholars have been unable to coordinate what Paul says about the various visits to Jerusalem in Galatians 1 with what Acts tells us about such visits.

Christian Leadership in Antioch

In any case, at the beginning of chapter 13 we are back at Antioch. Acts gives us a list of the leaders of the church in Antioch. This list includes five names, which Luke gives in the following order:
1. Barnabas
2. Simeon, who was called Niger
3. Lucius of Cyrene
4. Manaen, a member of the court of Herod
5. Saul

48

The first and the last name need no further identification, for Luke has already introduced them, and they become better known as the story unfolds. The second was probably called **Niger** because he was dark-skinned. This has led to the speculation that he may have also been from Cyrene like Lucius, and even that he may have been the Simon of Cyrene who was made to carry the cross behind Jesus (Luke 23:26 and the parallel passages in the other Gospel accounts). About **Lucius** no more is known. It has been suggested, but not generally accepted, that he may have been Luke, the writer of the Gospel and Acts. Finally, it has also been suggested that **Manaen** was the source for much of the detailed information about Herod's actions that the books of Luke and Acts give us. (Although Luke may not have been "Lucius," it is clear that he had a connection with the church in Antioch.)

The most important element in this entire section (at least to Luke) was recorded next: "The Holy Spirit said. . ." (13:2). Again, the point is that the entire enterprise to which most of the rest of Acts will be devoted was not of human design, but the result of the Spirit's guidance.

Dimension 3:
What Does the Bible Mean to Us?

Why the Focus on Antioch?

If we did not know the rest of the story, we would be surprised at all the time that Luke spent telling us about the church in Antioch. He had already written of the beginnings of a number of new Christian communities, and this passage seems to be more of the same. Rather than spending time reading about the church in Antioch, and about newly arrived characters such as Saul, Simon, Niger, and Lucius of Cyrene, we may be eager to get back to Jerusalem, and to find out what was happening there. After all, Jerusalem was the center of the action! It was there that the apostles lived. That was the church where it all began, and the church from which leadership had always been provided.

Luke spent all this time telling about the church in Antioch, because very soon the center of the action would shift from Jerusalem to Antioch. We may be curious to know what happened to Peter, to John, and to the rest of the apostles. Luke, however, was more interested in showing how the Holy Spirit constantly moved the church across new horizons. To see new horizons one has to shift one's vantage point.

A SHIFT IN VANTAGE POINTS

What happened, in brief, is that the old center, Jerusalem, soon lost its privileged position. The center of early church action moved to faraway Antioch, three hundred miles distant. From this point on, Luke centered his attention on the work of the church in Antioch, not because it was the oldest church or the richest, but because it had become a new center for mission.

This movement to the "fringes" has happened throughout the history of the church. Note that most of the New Testament was not written in Jerusalem (if, in fact, any of it was written there), but rather in the mission field. The New Testament was written at the "edge," where belief met with unbelief, where the church had to face new issues, and where, therefore, it was necessary to be creative. Perhaps Christians in Jerusalem did not like it, but that is how it was to be. Later, the great centers of learning were in Paris, Oxford, and southern Europe. But the initial impulse for reformation, came from a small university town at what was then seen as the fringes of civilization. Again, people in Rome and in Paris did not like it.

Today many of us stand in a similar situation. Our churches have long been the center of mission. It has been up to us to preach the gospel in various parts of the world. Missionaries from our churches founded churches in India, in China, in the former Belgian Congo, and on Pacific islands.

Today that is no longer the case. In each of these places there are strong Christian churches with local leadership. Many of those churches are growing rapidly— much more rapidly than most churches in the United States. They are asking new questions about mission in today's world, and responding to their own challenges in innovative ways, some of which may seem strange to us. Churches founded and nourished by western missionaries are now sending missionaries to the rest of the world, including the United States.

What are we to do? One option is to grieve for the past when we provided the lion's share of Christian leadership. Another option, based on the first, is to try to thwart the leadership of Christians in other parts of the world. But would this not be tantamount to denying our missionaries their greatest achievement: the planting of churches that no longer need to look to us for leadership and direction?

A better option is to recognize the work of the Holy Spirit in all modern "Antiochs," to rejoice that there are now so many new centers of mission and evangelism.

Mission Moves in Many Directions

If you look again at the text, you will note that eventually mission moved in both directions. Antioch received the gospel from Jerusalem; and when there was famine in Jerusalem Antioch collected an offering for them.

Today, mission is once again moving in dual directions. The church in the United States provided personnel and financial resources to a number of churches in various parts of the world. Now some of those churches are beginning to offer some of their expertise in evangelism and some of their profound spirituality as a resource within the United States.

Isn't this what mission is all about? It is about creating a worldwide church that, like the early community in Jerusalem, provides support for those in need, whatever the need may be.

Finally, the text tells us all that the Holy Spirit is constantly calling us to new adventures of faith. In a way, this is the central thesis of the entire Book of Acts. To those who felt that the church had made a mistake by becoming an increasingly Gentile community, Acts responded that this move was made under the guidance of the Holy Spirit. To those who feared the future, Acts insisted on the promise of the power of the Spirit, who would be with the disciples to the ends of the earth. Throughout history, this has been one of the most difficult lessons for the church to learn. Someone has said that the seven last words of the church will be: "We've never done it that way before!"

New Adventures in Faith

Can you think of new adventures of faith to which the Holy Spirit may be calling you or your church today? If so, have you prayed about it? Have you asked your congregation to pray about it? Are you and your congregation willing to hear what the Spirit has to say to you today, and do it?

Dimension 4:
A Daily Bible Journey Plan

> *Day 1:* Acts 12:6-19
> *Day 2:* Acts 12:20-25
> *Day 3:* Acts 13:1-3
> *Day 4:* Acts 13:4-12
> *Day 5:* Acts 13:13-41
> *Day 6:* Acts 13:42-52
> *Day 7:* Acts 14:1-7

Acts 13:13-52

7 JEALOUSY AND JOY

What to Watch For

We are now in the middle of Paul's first missionary journey. This journey is covered in Acts 13 and 14. As you read, watch for the following emphases:

➤ In these two chapters, Luke gives us only highlights of what happened in a few of the places that Paul and Barnabas visited: Cyprus, Antioch of Pisidia, Iconium, and Lystra. In between there must have been many other incidents worth noting. Luke, however, was not interested in giving us a chronicle of all that happened. Rather, he chose to select a few incidents that he underscored in order to make a point, or to give us an idea of how the mission developed. This idea is quite clear in the passage we are studying.

➤ Here we have a fairly long speech put on the lips of Paul (13:16-41). From that point on, except in exceptional circumstances where the audience is quite different, Acts only gives us a few lines as a summary of Paul's sermons. This omission of detail means that in these other situations we are to understand that what Paul said was more or less the same as what he said in Antioch of Pisidia.

➤ Thus, the passage we are studying was Luke's best summary of Paul's preaching in the synagogues he visited in his travels.

1. Where and when did Paul give the speech quoted here?

2. What was the first reaction of those who heard him? Did that attitude change? Why?

3. Does the story have a "happy ending"?

Missionary Travels

As you begin reading this passage, you may wish to look at the map on page 112, and see where Paul and Barnabas were. Note that the passage begins with the missionaries leaving Paphos (in Cyprus, to which the previous passage refers) and takes them eventually to Antioch in Pisidia. (See

photo, page 53.) Along the route at Pamphylia, John Mark decided to return to Jerusalem (see also Acts 15:38), and Paul and Barnabas continued to Antioch.

This is not the Antioch from which they had left, but a much smaller city in the heart of Asia Minor, part of the Roman province of Galatia (as were also the other cities mentioned later in the same chapter: Iconium, Lystra, and Derbe). It had some commercial importance, since it sat on the road that crossed Anatolia from the East towards Ephesus. Today, all that is left are some ruins which few tourists visit.

Luke told us nothing of the activities of Paul and Barnabas before the particular sabbath in which his narrative began. Judging by the way the story begins, it was possible that they had already been in Antioch for some time, and that this was not their first sabbath there.

A Word of Consolation

In any case, on this particular occasion the two were invited to speak. It is interesting to note that literally what they were invited to give is "a word of consolation" (15). Earlier, we were told that Barnabas' name means "son of consolation." Yet, Luke told us nothing about what Barnabas said. Instead, he centered his attention on Paul's speech.

Paul's Speech in Antioch

Paul began his speech after the manner of a classic orator, standing up and asking for silence with a gesture. (Usually, speakers at the synagogue simply sat.) He then offered a speech that can be clearly divided into three sections:

➤ 13:16-25
➤ 13:26-37
➤ 13:38-41

The speech was addressed to those present in the synagogue. Those present included the "Israelites" (16) as well as "others who fear God" (26).

The first part of the speech was a brief summary of the history of Israel. One verse (17) deals with the election of Israel and all the subsequent history up to the escape from Egypt. The next verse (18) tells of the wanderings in the wilderness. Two more verses (19-20) summarize the conquest of the land and the period of the judges. In that incredibly rapid survey, we may be surprised to find that an entire verse (21) deals with King Saul—until we remember that the speaker was named after that king, and that, like that first king of Israel, he too was of the tribe of Benjamin. The report that Saul reigned "forty years" is not to be found elsewhere in the Bible. Apparently it was part of common Jewish tradition at the time, for it is found also in the writings of another Jewish author (Josephus). Finally, the brief survey of the history of Israel was brought to its culmination in the story of David in verse

22. Up to this time, Paul has scarcely said anything that his audience did not already know, since they were all Jews or at least *God-fearers*.

It is in verse 23 that Paul introduced something radically new, which must have jolted his audience. (One can almost imagine the audience yawning at this long-winded rabbi telling them what they had heard from the cradle, and then suddenly sitting bolt upright!) Unexpectedly, Paul leaped over the centuries. He said nothing of Solomon or the division of the kingdom, nor of the exile and return, or the more recent struggles at the time of the Maccabees. From David, he leaped to the immediate past: "Of this man's [David's] posterity God has brought to Israel a Savior, Jesus, as he promised" (23).

Oddly, Paul said little about the life and teachings of Jesus. Rather, he completed this first part of his speech by focusing on the last of the many prophets who foretold the coming of Jesus, John the Baptist. Quite likely, many in his audience would have already heard of John, and thus Paul connected what he was telling them about Jesus with what they already knew.

The second part of the speech (verses 26-37) began with another address to the audience. The first began with "You Israelites" (literally, in Greek, *"Men, Israelites"*); the second began with "my brothers" (or, in another possible translation, *"my brothers and sisters"*). Here again Paul addressed both constituencies among his audience: those who were "descendants of Abraham's family" and the "others who fear God" (26).

This second section focuses on Jesus' death and resurrection. The argument was basically that, since the Jews in Jerusalem—and particularly their leaders—had rejected Jesus, the message had been sent to others who were far away. The reason for this was the attitude of the leaders in Jerusalem toward the prophecies that announced the coming of the Messiah. They failed to recognize Jesus, or to understand "the words of the prophets that are read every sabbath" (27). Precisely because they did not understand the prophecies, they fulfilled them by turning Jesus over to the Romans for his condemnation. It was for this reason that the rest of this second section of the speech focused on prophecies that applied to Jesus. In essence, what Paul was saying was "Don't do what those leaders in Jerusalem did. Listen to the prophets, and you will believe that Jesus is the one they announced."

The third section of the speech (verses 38-41) begins with another direct address to the audience: "my brothers" (verse 38). This was an exhortation to believe the message, as well as a further clarification of the message itself. It was here that the speech introduced the typically Pauline theme of the impossibility of salvation through obedience to the law and the need for salvation by grace, through Jesus: "By this Jesus everyone who believes is set free from all those sins from which you could not be freed by the law of Moses" (29).

Finally, the speech ended with a further reference to a prophecy that warned Paul's listeners not to do what the leaders in Jerusalem did, lest they fulfill the prophecy by becoming the scoffers to whom the prophecy referred.

The Response of the Audience

The response of the audience was quite positive. Those who were present at the synagogue urged Paul and Barnabas to continue speaking to them on the next sabbath. (Note that apparently both Paul and Barnabas spoke, although Luke recorded only Paul's speech.) Others followed Paul and Barnabas, "who spoke to them and urged them to continue in the grace of God" (43).

The impact of the message was such that the next sabbath, that is, a week later, "almost the whole city gathered to hear the word of the Lord" (44). Acts records that "when the Jews saw the crowds, they were filled with jealousy" (45). Apparently what this means is that this Jewish community, which was quite content to welcome Gentile "God-fearers" at its meetings in the synagogue, and which was also quite positive toward the message proclaimed by Paul and Barnabas, changed its mind when it realized that the consequence of such preaching would be that the promises made to Abraham would now be made available, not just to a few "God-fearers," but practically to an entire Gentile city. Consequently, they began to oppose and contradict what Paul and Barnabas were saying. As a response to that attitude, the missionaries turned to the Gentiles, again quoting Scripture to justify their decision. The result was that the Gentiles "were glad and praised the word of the Lord" (48) and many were converted.

The Word of the Lord Spread Throughout the Region

Luke did not tell us how long the missionaries remained in Antioch of Pisidia. It must have been a relatively long time, since "the word of the Lord spread throughout the region" (49).

After some time, however, the Jews of the city managed to incite "the devout women [that is, God-fearers or sympathizers with Judaism] of high standing and the leading men of the city" (50). Paul and Barnabas were driven out of the region. Note that here, as in the earlier chapters of Acts, it was the elite, "women of high standing" (50) and "the leading men of the city" (50) that opposed the preaching of the gospel. In earlier chapters, it was the Jewish elite of Jerusalem. Here, it is the Gentile (but some of them "Godfearing") elite of Antioch. Apparently, the populace of the city remained favorable to the preaching of the missionaries.

Forced to leave the city, Paul and Barnabas shook the dust off their sandals and went to Iconium, where, according to Acts 14:1, "the same thing occurred."

This development, however, did not destroy the faith of those in Antioch who had believed. One would expect the story to end in a note of sadness or anger that the missionaries had to leave and for an entirely unfounded reason. Instead, Acts closed its account of the events at Antioch of Pisidia by telling us that "the disciples were filled with joy and with the Holy Spirit" (52).

Identifying With the Story

It is easy for us to read a passage such as this, and begin by identifying ourselves with the heroes of the story, Paul and Barnabas. But before we do that it is important that we understand the "jealousy" of those Jews who first rejected the gospel and then organized things so that Paul and Barnabas would have to leave the city.

These Jews who so opposed the preaching of the gospel were religious people. They had kept their faith and traditions, probably in some cases after several generations of being away from the land of their ancestors. Doing so would have been no easy matter, especially in a society in which so much of trade and daily life was connected with the worship of many and sundry gods. Trade guilds were often organized as religious groups with a patron god who protected the interests of the group and in whose worship the guild expressed its unity. Thus, any good Jews would automatically be excluded from such a guild—and from the trade connected with it. Local festivals often centered on sacrifices to the deities of the place as well as on banquets in which the meat of the sacrifices was consumed. Therefore, in order to keep themselves pure as true Jews, the people in a Jewish community, such as that in Antioch, had to be very committed and ready to make a number of sacrifices.

Resentments and Jealousies

Taking those facts into account, it is not difficult to see why such people would be jealous of their faith and their traditions and would be eager to defend both against any encroachment or innovation. One can also understand how such a community would have developed a sense of privilege, a feeling that there was something special and unique about them.

Thus, when Paul and Barnabas came announcing that the promised Messiah had come, these good Jews rejoiced and were eager to hear more about it. When they discovered that this news meant that all these Gentiles, many of whom had often polluted themselves with the worship of idols and with unclean food, were also invited to join the people of God, they resented it.

It is important for us to understand this situation, for as believers we often face the same danger. In fact, the more religious we are, the more real the danger! It is not easy to be a Christian in today's world. Probably our difficulties are not as great as those faced by Jews in Antioch of Pisidia in the first century; however, they are just as real. We live in a society that lives by values that often contradict Christian values—getting ahead, winning even at the expense of others, avoiding pain at all costs, making and spending as much as possible, using violence as an easy solution for conflict. It takes a special effort to remain faithful in such a society. Therefore, as a means to strengthen our resolve, we tend to emphasize our uniqueness and the contrast between "us" and the rest of the world.

There is value in doing so, for otherwise we might easily succumb to the subtle temptations of today's world. There is also a danger. The danger is that, like those Jews in Antioch, we might become so proud of our religion, of our traditions, of our own religiosity, that we may become jealous of those others whom God may be calling and inviting to join us as God's people. It is for this reason that, like the Jews in Antioch of Pisidia, the church has often been unable to welcome others as God intends—and thus has been unfaithful to its calling.

Imagine a Common Situation

Imagine a fairly common situation in our day. Yours is a church that has stood in the middle of the city for generations. Your grandparents were married in this building. You and your children were baptized here. Every room and every window remind you of something or someone now gone. To you and to most of your congregation, this particular church is the center of your religious life as well as of much of your social life.

Now the population of the area is changing. Many of the members of the congregation have moved away and continue coming to church only on Sundays, because the distance is too great to travel every day—and in any case the area is no longer "safe" at night. A new ethnic group is moving into your community. The pastor and a few of the members of the church have begun inviting these new arrivals. They have organized a basketball league and a daycare center. Many of the new group are becoming members of the church. Changes are afoot! Their food is different from yours, and on Sunday mornings when you visit the recreation hall, there are odors to which you are not accustomed. They are bringing strange music into the worship service. They have no understanding of those people memorialized in the beautiful stained-glass windows that you so love.

How would you react? How do you think most of the congregation would react? What course of action would you recommend?

Do you now understand a little better why those Jews in Antioch of Pisidia reacted the way they did?

Imagine Yourself as a Newcomer

Turn the story around. Imagine that you are one of the newcomers. Imagine that you have come to church and found faith and hope in it. You have also found opposition and strife. Eventually, the pastor who began this new outreach is driven out by those who resent it. What would be your reaction? Would you become bitter and disillusioned? Or would you be able to retain the joy of the gospel?

Go back and read the very last verse of the passage we are studying. Think again about the question posed at the beginning of the lesson: Does the story have a "happy ending"?

Dimension 4: A Daily Bible Journey Plan

> *Day 1:* Acts 14:8-20
>
> *Day 2:* Acts 14:21-28
>
> *Day 3:* Acts 15:1-11
>
> *Day 4:* Acts 15:12-21
>
> *Day 5:* Acts 15:22-35
>
> *Day 6:* Acts 15:36-41
>
> *Day 7:* Acts 16:1-5

Acts 15:1-35

8 JERUSALEM

What to Watch For

In earlier lessons we have seen that one of Luke's concerns was Jewish Christians who were not convinced that the Gentile mission had been a good idea—or who at least thought that Gentile converts to Christianity should be required to obey all the law. Historians often refer to people holding such opinions as *Judaizers*.

The episode that we are about to study is often called "The Council at Jerusalem." As you read, watch for the following:

➤ In telling the story of the Council at Jerusalem, Luke was acknowledging that there were indeed people in the early church who felt as the Judaizers did. He was also acknowledging that such people had a rightful place in the church.

➤ Luke recorded that even the so-called Judaizers eventually agreed that all the requirements of the law should not be imposed on Gentile converts to Christianity.

1. List a "cast of characters" in this story. Do you have a fairly clear idea of what each of them stood for?

2. Do you think that there is any connection between the fact that Paul and Barnabas had been on an extended missionary journey and their being named among the delegation to go to Jerusalem?

What Shall Be Done With the Gentiles?

Acts does not tell us how soon after the return of Paul and Barnabas these events took place. The previous chapter ends by telling us that "they stayed there [in Antioch] with the disciples for some time" (14:28). This chapter begins: "Then certain individuals . . ." (1). It is not clear whether the people who went from Judea to Antioch did so because they had learned of the mission of Paul and Barnabas to the Gentiles or for some other reason.

In any case, their message was quite clear: Gentile Christians must obey all the law of Moses. This message was summarized in a statement regarding circumcision: "Unless you are circumcised according to the custom of Moses, you cannot be saved" (1).

So far, Acts has not clarified the practice of the church in Antioch, or of Paul and Barnabas, regarding the Gentiles. Yet, since there is no indication in the narrative that Gentiles were required to obey the entire law, and since Gentiles were readily added to the church, the clear implication is that there was no such requirement. We know from the letters of Paul that this was indeed the case. That is a point that he had to make and defend repeatedly. Therefore, as could have been expected, "Paul and Barnabas had no small dissension and debate with them" (2). The eventual result was that a delegation was sent to

Jerusalem to discuss the issues involved with the leaders of that church. The delegation consisted of Paul, Barnabas, and some others from the church in Antioch.

Great Joy to All Believers

Along the way, through Phoenicia and Samaria, they brought the news of the conversion of the Gentiles, which "brought great joy to all the believers" (3)—a detail that Luke probably included in order to indicate that the mission to the Gentiles had widespread acceptance.

In Jerusalem, however, there was not total agreement on the matters under discussion. According to Acts, the majority of the church and its leadership welcomed them, but there were "some believers who belonged to the sect of the Pharisees" (5) who objected, holding to the position of the Judaizers who had gone to Antioch.

We may find it surprising that the church in Jerusalem, after the episode of Cornelius and the church's joyful reaction in Acts 10 and 11, had to revisit what was essentially the same question. In this respect, Luke showed an understanding of how human groups work and make decisions. A decision was made in the light of a situation or event (in this case, the conversion of Cornelius). Time passed. That very decision had to be reaffirmed when challenged by other events (in this case, the conversion of a greater number of Gentiles). Thus, instead of being "confused," as some commentators have claimed, Luke's description of the process seems eminently realistic.

Luke was not explicit, but the order of the story implies that there were several meetings, probably over a period of several days. In 15:4, the delegation from Antioch was welcomed "by the church and the apostles and the elders," to whom was given an account of "all that God had done with them." In verse 6, it was "the apostles and elders" who gathered to consider the matter. Yet in verse 12 "the whole assembly" kept silence and apparently listened to another report from Barnabas and Paul. Finally, in verse 22, "the apostles and the elders" made a decision "with the consent of the whole church." Thus, it would appear that Luke telescoped into a very brief narrative what may well have been a process of days or even longer.

Who Should Bear the Burden of the Law?

After some time, Peter intervened in the discussion. He reminded his listeners of the conversion of Cornelius and how he had been chosen by God to be the first to take the message to the Gentiles. He concluded that the burden of the law, which the Jews themselves found impossible to bear (that is, to obey fully) should not be placed on the neck of these new disciples.

Luke dramatically told us that "the whole assembly kept silence" (12) and listened to a full report on the conversion of the Gentiles from Barnabas and Paul. Obviously, a similar report had already been given. What Luke implied was that, on the basis of Peter's words, earlier reports were given fuller credence. Note that Luke reverted to the order he had changed during the course of the Gentile mission. When they first appeared in his story, Luke referred to these two as "Barnabas and Paul"; later, during their missionary journey, Paul took the lead. They were referred to then as "Paul and Barnabas." Here, they were again referred to as "Barnabas and Paul." This is an important detail. In Jerusalem, where he was known and had gained the trust of the apostles, Barnabas was a more important figure than Paul.

Later on, as you continue your journey through the Bible, you will note that one of Paul's typical themes is the burden of the law upon Gentile believers. Thus, what Luke attempted to underscore was the agreement of the apostles, and in particular of Peter, with Paul and his theology.

James intervened in the discussion, supporting Peter's position and adding scriptural proof. He suggested that four things were to be demanded of Gentile converts:

➤ that they abstain from things polluted by idols
➤ and from fornication
➤ and from whatever had been strangled
➤ and from blood (20)

Was this an agreeable solution? Apparently so. A letter was sent not only to Antioch but also "to the believers of Gentile origin in Antioch and Syria and Cilicia" (23), listing the same four points that James had suggested. This letter was sent back to Antioch with the delegation that had come, led by Paul and Barnabas, but also with two representatives from the church in Jerusalem—Judas, called Barsabbas, and Silas.

That letter also took any authority away from the Judaizers who had gone to Antioch, declaring that these were "certain persons who have gone out from us, though with no instructions from us" (24).

Silas went with Paul on his next missionary journey. How Silas came to be back in Antioch, Luke did not bother to tell us. After all, he was not telling the story of individuals and their doings, but rather the story of how the Holy Spirit had brought the church to where it is today.

How Much of the Law Must a Gentile Obey?

Upon receipt of the letter, the congregation in Antioch gathered for its reading with much rejoicing at the results of the discussion in Jerusalem. Judas and Silas, both "prophets"—that is, preachers—strengthened the believers in Antioch and then returned to Jerusalem.

In order to understand the discussion and the decisions made at this meeting in Jerusalem, we must try to place ourselves at that time and in those circumstances and try to see matters from the perspective of that early Jewish church. As we look at those events, we tend to think that what was happening was that a large number of Jews was abandoning Judaism in favor of Christianity. But when *they* looked at the situation, what they saw was that a large number of Gentiles were now claiming the promises made to Abraham and his descendants, and that they were making this claim through Jesus Christ (that is, Jesus the Messiah, for that is the meaning of the word *Christ*). Therefore, the question that was being posed was not, as we would think today, *How much of the law must one obey in order to be a Christian?* The question was rather, *How much of the law must a Gentile obey in order to be admitted to life in the midst of Israel?*

When the question is phrased in those terms, it seems clear that what James was doing was simply insisting on the ancient laws that were to be applied to aliens residing in the midst of Israel.

LAWS PERTAINING TO ALIENS

Laws pertaining to aliens residing in the midst of Israel were spelled out in Leviticus 17:8–18:30. Although the list, as it appeared in Acts, consisted of four elements, there were three essential parts to this legislation.

➤ First, aliens residing within Israel had to abandon their idolatrous practices as well as all that was connected with them. This was essentially what was meant by James' first stipulation.

➤ Second, they had to abstain from sexual immorality. This was the meaning of *fornication*, the second of James' stipulations. This was not just sexual intercourse outside of marriage, but included a number of other sexual practices as listed in Leviticus 18.

➤ Thirdly, there were the dietary laws. Of these, the most important was not to eat blood. Blood was considered the very life of an animal. Among many ancient people, it was thought that by eating an animal's blood one ate its spirit and acquired its characteristics. Thus, the law not to eat blood was a sign of respect for life. Killing was necessary in order to eat and thus to live; but killing must not entail disrespect for the life that was given in exchange for ours. For that reason, Jewish dietary laws required that an animal be bled. And that was what in essence James said in his third and fourth stipulations: to abstain from anything that had been strangled.

The Reign of God Was at Hand

One of the most interesting elements in this story—and one that we often miss—is that those who most stringently opposed Paul were Pharisees who had become Christians, as had Paul himself.

It was easy to understand why these people objected to the mission to the Gentiles, unless it involved requiring Gentile converts to be circumcised and to keep the full law of Moses. Among the Jewish sects of the time, the Pharisees were noted precisely for their careful attention to the law and its requirements. They objected to the facile religiosity of other Jews, who were content with a general obedience to the main points of the law. Fasting, praying, the dietary laws, and certainly the sabbath rest, were carefully regulated and observed by the Pharisees.

When these people embraced Christianity—that is, when they came to believe that Jesus was indeed the Messiah promised by Scripture—they did not necessarily relax their strict observance of the law. On the contrary, since Jesus was indeed the Messiah, then the Reign of God was at hand. This recognition was reason for stricter observance, rather than being reason for laxity. Thus, they were naturally disturbed by a preaching or practice that allowed Gentiles to join the people of the promise without also taking upon themselves the obligation of being obedient to the law.

If the attitude of these Pharisees was not surprising, Paul's certainly was. He too had been a Pharisee—and a zealous one at that (see Philippians 3:4-6). Presumably he had been as zealous for the law as any Pharisee. Yet he defended a position diametrically opposed to that of the Pharisees. How are we to explain that difference?

We might be inclined to say that this was the result of Paul's experience of conversion. But then, if these other Pharisees had joined the church, it must have been because they too had a conversion or some experience that led them to take this position so unpopular among their own people.

Probably the difference came from another source. These Pharisees in Jerusalem had heard and accepted the Gospel; but Paul, besides receiving the message, had joined God's mission in the world. These Pharisees had joined the community; but the church in Antioch, and then Paul and Barnabas, had done more. They engaged in mission to reach others.

The difference between Paul and these Pharisees was that they had not lived through Paul's experiences in Antioch, preaching to the Gentiles and accepting them into the communion of the church. They had not had the experiences of Antioch of Pisidia, of Iconium, and of Lystra.

Certainly the Holy Spirit was active in Jerusalem. Acts gives ample proof of that. The Spirit was opening the way to a new reality in those other places where Paul and Barnabas had been. Therefore, when the question of the conversion of the Gentiles was posed in Jerusalem, Paul and Barnabas saw the action of God among the Gentiles in a way that these Pharisees found hard to comprehend.

The Growing Edge

The same has been true throughout the history of the church. There is much truth in the phrase "the growing edge." We often think that it is the center that is most important and the center that provides leadership for the rest. The opposite is often the case. It is the "growing edge," those places where the church is encountering new situations and seeking to be faithful in them, that most often provides a new vision, a new impetus, a new life.

A Mission of Outreach and Love

And what has been true in the past is also true today. We tend to think that the most important leadership in the life of the church is in the general boards and agencies, or in bishops' offices. The truth is that the real leadership of the church is wherever Christians are engaged in mission.

Look at your own church. What is most important in the life of your church? You may be inclined to think that your church's budget or its building or its interesting speakers at Wednesday night suppers are most important. All these are important. They are important, however, only to the degree that they empower you and others for mission. If all that they do is entertain, they are missing the mark. Even if they sustain you and the other members of the church in your religious life, if that is all they do, they are still missing the mark. All of these things are there to support the real mission of the church, which is one of outreach to others in witness and love.

Suppose that your church were suddenly to realize that the true reason for its existence was its outreach beyond the borders of faith. In other words, suppose that your church were suddenly to become a radically missionary and evangelistic church. There is no telling what changes might take place—probably changes as fundamental and as exciting as those that turned the Pharisee Paul into the apostle to the Gentiles.

Why wait for the entire church to take this step? Paul and the Christians in Antioch did not wait for the decision in Jerusalem before they launched their missionary outreach. Suppose that you yourself stop reading for a moment and ask God to empower and to send you as an arm of the church to reach those who are outside. Or suppose that you and a few others covenant in prayer to look around yourselves and around your church for those who do not know the joys of the gospel. You will be surprised at what you will learn from them even as you witness to them! That was Paul's experience among the Gentiles. That was Peter's experience with Cornelius. That too can be your experience.

Dimension 4:
A Daily Bible Journey Plan

Day 1: Acts 16:6-10

Day 2: Acts 16:11-15

Day 3: Acts 16:16-24

Day 4: Acts 16:25-40

Day 5: Acts 17:1-9

Day 6: Acts 17:10-15

Day 7: Acts 17:16-34

THENS

What to Watch For

In today's passage, the preaching of the gospel encounters Greek philosophy for the first time. That is probably what makes it most significant. As you read, watch for the following emphases:

➤ Until this point, most of those who have heard the preaching of the gospel were either Jews or "God-fearers"—that is, sympathizers of Judaism. Also there has been some contact with Roman officials as in the case of Sergius Paulus, the proconsul to whom Paul and Barnabas spoke at Paphos in Cyprus (see Acts 13:6-11).

➤ Paul has come to the very capital of Greek philosophy and culture and has the opportunity to present the gospel to people there. Since this was an entirely different circumstance from the many others in which Paul spoke at the synagogue, Acts gives us an outline of his speech.

➤ Paul's speech and its results have been much debated. Throughout the centuries one of the most difficult issues that the church has had to face, and one of the most debated, has been precisely the question of the relationship between the gospel and human culture.

1. Why was Paul in Athens? Who was with him? What was he doing there?

2. Why was he taken to the Areopagus?

3. What was the gist of his message?

4. What was the response?

Dimension 2:
What Does the Bible Mean?

Forced to Flee, Paul Testifies in Athens

Paul had been forced to flee from Beroea, while for unknown reasons Silas and Timothy were left behind. Apparently, the trip from Beroea to Athens was by land, for a voyage by sea would not have required the company (one might even say the escort) of a group of believers from Beroea. Having delivered Paul safely in Athens, the delegation from Beroea returned home, leaving Paul there to wait until Silas and Timothy could join him.

If you read further on, you will see that Timothy and Silas did not join Paul until much later, after Paul had left Athens. The three met again in Corinth. (See Acts 18:5.)

Although Paul was not in Athens in order to preach, but simply to wait for his companions, that did not keep him from his usual activities. "He argued in the synagogues with the Jews and the devout persons" (17)—that is, the "God-fearers." In this particular case, however, there was an added factor. Athens was not just any city with its few temples devoted to the local gods. Athens was both an important place of traditional pagan worship and a center of philosophical and intellectual debate.

ATHENS OF THE FIRST CENTURY

Traditional Pagan Worship

The Acropolis of Athens (that is to say, the "high city" in which many of the temples were clustered) is still one of the most magnificent sets of ruins from antiquity. At that time, these temples were not in ruins. Yet the entire province of Greece was impoverished and its population depleted. Thus, Athens would have been a city with an inordinate number of temples for the size of its population. As a Jew and as a Christian, it is not surprising that Paul "was deeply distressed to see that the city was full of idols" (16).

Athenian Philosophy and Culture

To this day, the very name *Athens* is a synonym of knowledge and wisdom. It was here that Socrates and Plato had flourished. Indeed, the academy that Plato had founded was still flourishing. The statues that adorned the temples and public places were the work of famous sculptors, such as Phidias. In the theaters plays by Euripides and Aristophanes were common fare.

Although Plato was the most important philosopher that Athens ever produced, by the middle of the first century the dominant philosophy in Athens was no longer **Platonism**, but, as Acts correctly tells us, **Epicureanism** and **Stoicism**. Much of this philosophy, however, was no longer the profound thought of Socrates and Plato, but rather a superficial debate of people who, as Acts says, "would spend their time in nothing but telling or hearing something new" (17:21).

We are told it is for all these reasons that Paul argued in the synagogue with Jews and God-fearers. Just as importantly, Paul argued "in the marketplace every day with those who happened to be there" (17). This "marketplace" was probably the main *agora* of the city, whose ruins can still be seen—although it could also be one of the many squares in Athens. There he would find himself debating with Gentiles who held to the worship of the traditional gods. He also found himself debating with philosophers of the two leading schools: **Epicureans** and **Stoics**.

Paul Called a "Babbler"

What the Epicureans and Stoics said about Paul was not very flattering. They call him a "babbler" (18). The word that they employed originally referred to birds that went about scratching the earth looking for seeds. It was applied to people who collected rags in the city dumps! In this passage, the word means someone who, like a bird that scratches for seeds or someone poking around for rags, collects loose bits of information from here and there, thus sounding very wise but knowing nothing. In other words, the Epicureans and Stoics had called Paul a *dilettante*!

"Others"—probably not the philosophers, but the less attentive among the populace—decided that Paul was "a proclaimer of foreign divinities" (18). The reason they gave, and which Acts reports, was utterly ridiculous: Paul spoke of Jesus and the Resurrection. Since in Greek *resurrection* is a feminine term, evidently these people thought that Paul was preaching a pair of new gods.

Paul Preaches in the Areopagus

Apparently, however, the curiosity about what Paul was teaching came to the point that he was brought to the Areopagus, the place where the ancient court of Athens had gathered.

The Areopagus was a rocky outcrop that from ancient times had been a place for deliberations. Today, a bronze plaque at its foot quotes the entire text of Paul's speech there.

From the Areopagus, Paul could see the marketplace where he had been debating, and many of the temples that had caused him so much chagrin. Looking in the other direction, he would see, high above the Parthenon, several of the other temples in Athens.

71

At the Areopagus Paul responded to questions with his famous speech about "the unknown god" (23 and following). As was customary at that time, the speech began with words that flattered the audience, except that in this case, knowing Paul's understanding of such matters, we see that such flattery was somewhat tongue-in-cheek: "Athenians, I see how extremely religious you are in every way. For as I went through the city and looked carefully at the objects of your worship, I found among them an altar with the inscription, 'To an unknown God' " (22-23).

Paul Accuses Athenians of Ignorance

This introduction has sometimes been interpreted as if Paul were acknowledging the correctness of Athenian religiosity. In fact what we have here is a fine irony, which soon turned the tables on the Athenians and accused them of ignorance. Indeed, immediately after these words Paul continued: "What therefore you worship as unknown, this I proclaim to you" (23). Paraphrasing Paul's remarks may help us understand the magnitude of Paul's remarks: "I have come to cure your ignorance that you yourselves have confessed in this inscription." Paul continued his attack by saying the true God, the creator of all things, "does not live in shrines made by human hands" (24). In other words, the true God did not live in any of the Athenians' beautiful temples. Nor was God "served by human hands" (25). In other words, all the Athenians' sacrifices were in vain.

The core of Paul's message was "God has overlooked the times of human ignorance" (30). In other words: "Yes, you were ignorant, as I have just shown and as you yourselves confessed in erecting an altar to the 'unknown' God." (In Greek, the words for *ignorance* and for *unknown* have the same root). Paul said that God, however, was ready to overlook that ignorance. There was something new. God commands "all people everywhere to repent, because he has fixed a day on which he will have the world judged in righteousness by a man [Jesus] whom he has appointed" (30-31). What is the guarantee of what Paul shared? The guarantee is that God has raised Jesus from the dead.

Paul lost his audience at precisely this point. Hearing him speak of the resurrection of the dead, "some scoffed" (32). In Greek philosophy, there was much talk of the immortality of the soul. In general, however, it was held that the body was like a prison for the soul. Therefore, the true life beyond death must have nothing to do with the body. The "babbler" spoke of a life after death that involved a resurrection of the body! To most of these philosophers, and to others who had been influenced by the same world view, that idea made no sense. Others, perhaps more polite, or perhaps simply more sardonic, said, "We will hear you again about this" (32)—the equivalent of an adult who puts off a child by promising to do something "one of these days."

That was the end of Paul's speech. It did not have the widespread initial acceptance that his speech in Antioch of Pisidia had received. Actually, the concluding remark in verse 33, "at that point Paul left them," implied that Paul simply gave up and left them, probably to the accompaniment of their jeers and catcalls. Even so, Paul's efforts in Athens were not entirely wasted.

Paul's Efforts Were Not a Waste

Luke said nothing about Jews who joined the church, as he told in other places. Yet, since we are told that Paul did speak in the synagogue, one may well imagine that, as on other occasions, this produced some results. Luke mentioned two converts by name: Dionysius the Areopagite and a woman named Damaris. He also added that there were "others with them" (34).

The Bible does not mention these people again. The title "Areopagite," probably meant that Dionysius was a member of that ancient court, which still met. Later, legends were woven around both Dionysius and Damaris. Those, however, have no basis in the Book of Acts.

Dimension 3:
What Does the Bible Mean to Us?

A Famous, Faithful Speech

This is one of Paul's most famous speeches. It had a chance of being one of his most successful. Even though some of his listeners thought he was a "babbler," at least they had invited him to speak at the place where they discussed the most profound questions. He had begun well with a word of commendation to his audience.

Paul had shown that he knew classical letters by quoting from a Greek poet and two Greek philosophers. Even the seemingly harsh words that he had said about the gods would have been generally well received, for this was essentially what the best Greek philosophers had said about their own gods. If he had stopped at verse 29, his listeners would have been favorably impressed by his wisdom and eloquence, and he might even have had a chance to address them again.

A Famous, Unsuccessful Speech

Paul did not. Instead of limiting himself to what his audience would probably like, Paul spoke of things that they were not quite as ready to accept. First of all, he moved from the general principles

In the ancient art of rhetoric, which Paul was obviously practicing here, one always attempted a commendation of one's audience. This was called the "gaining of good will."

73

that are true at all times and all places to the concrete and the present. For ages, philosophers had been saying that "we ought not to think that the deity is like gold, or silver, or stone, an image formed by the art and imagination of mortals" (29). This idea, however, was a general principle requiring no particular action. Paul, in contrast, brought all this in the present and made a direct demand on his audience. *"Now* [God] commands all people everywhere to repent" (30). In other words, the idea was no longer a general principle that the Athenians could accept and keep on living as before; it was an urgent demand that required a decision.

As if this were not enough to alienate his audience, Paul spoke about Jesus and his resurrection from the dead. Paul, who knew enough of Greek philosophy to be able to quote relatively obscure Stoic philosophers, must also have known that such ideas would not go over well with his audience.

Yet Paul said such things. Why? Because to say otherwise would have made Paul a successful speaker but a disobedient witness.

Are We Called to Be Faithful or Successful?

This principle is enormously important for us today. There is always the temptation to let popularity guide what we say. We are not called to be popular. We are not called to be successful. We are called to be faithful. Being a faithful Christian is not always compatible with being popular and successful. Have you ever felt a tension between the two? When such tension arises, in which direction do your decisions lean?

A key point in Paul's message is often overlooked: "From one ancestor [or blood] he made all nations to inhabit the whole earth" (26).

We live in times when the whole world seems divided by ethnic strife. In what used to be Yugoslavia, in several countries in Africa, in Sri Lanka, and in a dozen other places, ethnic violence has reached almost incredible proportions. Who among us is unaware of racism or the hatred and violence associated with it?

Paul, a member of a people that had a long tradition of referring to itself as "God's chosen people," declared that, after all, all humankind is related. We are all of the same blood, tantamount to saying that we are all of the same family.

We need to hear this message again and again. That other person whom we stereotype and then hate, is in fact a relative, a child of the same God who is also our parent. Paul's assertion is important. Paul declared that God made humankind "to inhabit the whole earth" (26).

Global Issues, Christian Concerns

We know that idolatry and sexual immorality are against the will of God. So is hatred and violence. Do we realize that, when the earth is polluted so that it cannot be inhabited, we are also violating God's will? There are

74

ever growing regions in the earth that are no longer fit to sustain either human or animal life. In some sections of the world, deforestation is producing rampant desertification. Lakes and rivers that used to team with fish are now sewers carrying both human and industrial waste. That is not the purpose for which God made both the earth and humankind.

Furthermore, when the earth is managed in such a way that some people have no earth on which to inhabit, we are violating God's will. The question of what we do with the land, how we distribute it, and how we leave it for future generations is central to the Christian faith.

Obviously, all of these matters are global in scope. Since they are so large, we tend to become discouraged and decide there is nothing we can do about them. Why tackle issues on which there is little hope of success?

The answer, once again, is that we are not to measure our actions by our success, but by our fidelity. Paul could have given a very successful speech; he chose instead to be faithful. When we tackle issues of global magnitude, we may or may not be successful. We can be faithful—and that is the most important of all.

Dimension 4:
A Daily Bible Journey Plan

Day 1: Acts 18:1-17

Day 2: Acts 18:18-23

Day 3: Acts 18:24-28

Day 4: Acts 19:1-10

Day 5: Acts 19:11-20

Day 6: Acts 19:21-41

Day 7: Acts 20:1-6

10 CORINTH

What to Watch For

As was said at the beginning of this study, one of Luke's concerns in writing the Book of Acts was the possibility that Roman authorities might take a negative stance towards Christianity. Persecution might ensue. Here, for the first time since his brief appearance before Sergius Paulus in Cyprus, we see Paul before a high Roman official. As you read, watch for the following emphases:

➤ In telling this story, Luke made it clear that the accusations against Christians were brought by Jews who rejected the Christian proclamation.

➤ The accusations had to do with nothing that Rome considered "a matter of crime or serious villainy" (14) but rather debated the interpretation and application of Jewish law.

➤ The implication that other accusations might be brought against Christians, at a later time, were equally baseless and should also be thrown out of court.

1. What do we learn from this text about the attitudes of Roman authorities toward Christianity?

2. What does the text say about where Paul lived and how he supported his ministry?

3. What was Paul's relationship with the synagogue in Corinth?

Paul Left Athens for Corinth

The story begins with Paul having left Athens for Corinth. For once, we are not told that Paul had to flee from a city! Indeed, we are given no indication why he decided to move on to Corinth instead of waiting for his companions in Athens, as previously agreed.

Adapted from *Bible Teacher Kit,* © 1994 by Abingdon Press

77

Corinth was strategically placed in the isthmus of its name, separating the Aegean Sea from the Adriatic and joining the Peloponese with the rest of Greece.

Corinth was not a seaport, but was in the middle of the isthmus with the port of Cenchreae toward the east on the Aegean, and the port of Lechaion toward the west on the Gulf of Corinth, which in turn opened on the Adriatic. Shipping goods from Cenchreae to Lechaion saved the long navigation around the Peloponese, and Corinth benefited from the trade that this produced. A system of pulleys allowed small ships to be dragged from one seaport to the other.

A few years after Paul's visit, Nero attempted to dig a canal across the isthmus; but the project was abandoned. A canal was completed in 1893. Since the road leading into the Peloponese from northern Greece also passed by Corinth, the city profited also from the land trade going north and south.

A City of Resistance and Debauchery

Corinth had played a leading role in the resistance against Roman conquest. As a result Corinth was completely destroyed by the Romans in 146 B.C. Its location was so strategic, however, that in A.D. 44 Julius Caesar ordered that it be rebuilt. This was less than a hundred years before Paul's visit.

Therefore, the city was relatively new with a large population of recent arrivals and still much construction going on.

You may wish to look up their names in a Bible concordance. Note that *Priscilla* is the same as *Prisca* to whom Paul referred in this more respectful form of the same name.

From ancient times, and again after its reconstruction, Corinth was known for its debauchery, to the point that a verb had been coined, *to corinthize*, which meant to behave as one saw fit, with no regard for customs or morals.

Such a setting must have been daunting even for one such as Paul, who later told the Corinthians that "I came to you in weakness and in fear and in much trembling" (1 Corinthians 2:3).

In that awesome setting, Paul made contact with Aquila and his wife Priscilla. Aquila was a Jew from Pontus (on the southern coast of what is now the Black Sea), who had been in Italy until Emperor Claudius ordered "all Jews" to leave Rome. We know of the imperial decree from Roman sources. It appears likely that what prompted Claudius to expel the Jews was the conflict and turmoil caused by Christian preaching. It is also probable that Aquila and Priscilla were already Christians and were among the Jewish Christians who had been compelled to leave Rome. Otherwise, it would have been difficult to explain how a Jew, who had been expelled from Rome because of Christian preaching, would have offered hospitality to Paul.

Although in this passage no more is said of Aquila and Priscilla, we learn from the rest of the New Testament that this couple—and probably Priscilla more than Aquila—were important leaders in the early Christian church.

Silas and Timothy Arrived From Macedonia

Acts informs us that by trade Paul was a tentmaker. Since tentmaking was also the occupation of this couple, he went to live and work with them.

Since he was working, it was only "every sabbath," (that is, when neither he nor Priscilla and Aquila were working) that Paul would go to the synagogue and "try to convince Jews and Greeks" (4). This phrase probably meant God-fearing Gentiles who attended the synagogue.

Finally, Silas and Timothy arrived from Macedonia. Apparently, they brought funds from the church in Philippi, to which Paul was always grateful for economic support. Later, Paul wrote to the Corinthians: "When I was with you and was in need, I did not burden anyone, for my needs were supplied by the friends who came from Macedonia" (2 Corinthians 11:9). Possibly this is also the meaning of the phrase in Acts 18:5: "Paul was occupied with proclaiming the word." Now that he had other funds, Paul did not have to work all the time; therefore he spent his time "proclaiming the word, testifying to the Jews that the Messiah was Jesus" (5).

Paul's Preaching Rejected

Eventually, as in so many other cases, the bulk of the Jewish population in Corinth rejected Paul's preaching. Paul "shook the dust from his clothes" (6) and sought the Gentiles. This did not mean, however, that he went far. On the contrary, he merely moved his preaching to a house right next to the synagogue, owned by Titius (or Titus) Justus. This Titius Justus was "a worshiper of God," (7) which is to say, a "God-fearer," one of the many Gentiles who was convinced of the theological truth of Jewish monotheism, but who was not ready to become a Jew himself. Even among the Jews Paul had significant success, for a man by the name of Crispus, "the official of the synagogue" (this was an official title, literally the "archsynagogos") "became a believer in the Lord, together with all his household" (8). The same was true of many other Corinthians, who also believed and were baptized (8). However, all must not have been easy, for Luke told of a vision Paul had (9-10) in which the Lord assured him of protection.

As a sort of summary, Luke shared that Paul stayed in Corinth a year and a half. Although this information appears in the middle of the passage regarding Paul's stay in Corinth, this does not mean that he stayed a year and a half after the events that have just been told. Rather, it means that Paul stayed in Corinth for a total of some eighteen months.

Remember the passage from First Corinthians (quoted earlier), to the effect that Paul was in Corinth with much fear and trembling.

Proconsuls were the highest officials in a province. The title, "proconsul," meant a representative of the consuls, who in turn were the highest of Roman officials. There were two consuls at a time with a term of office of one year. Most proconsuls were former consuls, and thus represented the highest Roman aristocracy.

Finally, the Jewish opponents of Christianity made their move—or at least, the one move that Acts records. There was now a new proconsul. This new proconsul, to whom Acts refers as Gallio, was Lucius Junius Gallio Annaeus, a man known to us also from Roman secular history.

Paul Brought Before Gallio's Court

Apparently, the anti-Christian Jewish leadership (remember, there were also many Jewish Christians, including Paul, Aquila, and Crispus) thought that the new proconsul would respond positively to an accusation against Christians. They, therefore, "brought" Paul before Gallio's court (whether by force or not is unclear) and accused him of "persuading people to worship God in ways that are contrary to the law" (13).

The accusation itself was specious. The "law" was Rome's most cherished principle. However, this was Roman law, not the law of Moses. Thus, although the implication was that Paul was somehow subverting Roman order, in fact, it could be understood in the sense that he was subverting Jewish practice. Conceivably they were hoping that Gallio, who represented a government that had recently acted against the disturbances created by Christians preaching in Rome, was ready to take similar action in Corinth, at least by expelling Paul from the city.

Gallio had none of that. He quickly perceived that this was a matter among Jews, which had to do with Jewish law. He threw the entire process out of court. He literally told them that this had to do, not with Roman law, but with "your own law" (15). Therefore they were to solve the matter themselves.

Remember that we said at the beginning of this study that, in the writing of Acts, one of the concerns that Luke may have had was the growing tension with Roman authorities and the impending threat of persecution. He dealt with that issue by showing that Lucius Junius Gallio Annaeus, a man whose memory was generally respected at the time that Luke was writing, had decided that Christians ought not to be persecuted. At the same time, however, Luke realistically painted a picture of a Roman aristocrat who believed that such matters were below his notice and who was not even attentive when someone was beaten right in front of his tribunal (17).

This last verse of our passage (17) is confusing. We have not been told who Sosthenes was. He was another "official of the synagogue." But who was beating him and why? Were the Gentiles beating him because he brought a false or weak case before the proconsul? Were the Jews beating him because, as their leader, he had failed them? Were they beating him because he too, like Crispus, had become a Christian? There is no way of knowing.

Dimension 3:
What Does the Bible Mean to Us?

Christian Preaching Led to Conflicts in Rome

The passage begins and ends with two references to the manner in which Roman civil authorities dealt with Christianity and some of the consequences of its preaching. In Rome, Christian preaching had led to conflicts with those Jews who did not accept the gospel. The emperor had expelled the lot from the city. Now in Corinth, those conflicts were brought before the civil court only to be thrown out as having no connection with matters on which the civil government had an interest. As Gallio put it, "if it were a matter of crime or serious villainy, I would be justified in accepting the complaint of you Jews; but since it is a matter of questions about words and names and your own law, see to it yourselves" (14-15). The result was that, right outside of Gallio's court, there was practically a riot, to which he seemingly paid no attention.

These two examples of the attitudes of Roman authorities, when confronted with Christianity and its preaching, parallel the way in which modern secular governments and societies deal with issues of religion.

Separation of Church and State

In our own society, the principle that stands above all such matters is the constitutional clause affirming the separation of church and state—or, more precisely, forbidding the establishment of religion by the state. Originally, that clause was conceived as a means to guarantee freedom of religion, so that no one religion or church could use the power of the state against another or to gain advantage over another. As time has gone by, however, it has also come to mean the freedom from all religion, so that in theory religious considerations should be left out of the political decision-making process. In other words, in the words of Gallio, religious impulses are "questions about words and names and your own law" and therefore ought to be thrown out of the public arena.

The problem is that, even if Gallio had been right, his own decision not to hear the case led to a case in which he should have intervened—the beating of Sosthenes right in front of his own tribunal. A society, no matter how secular, may try to disengage itself from religious issues and motivations. Religious impulses are so strong, however, that they cannot really be ignored.

The same is true from the religious standpoint. You may decide that your religion ought not to become involved in your politics. But that is possible only if your religion is quite tame and irrelevant. If religion is vibrant, it will naturally become involved in everything that is important to society, including matters such as welfare reform, health reform, crime and punishment, and international relations. You may disagree with other people of equally intense and sincere religious motivation; you will not be able to keep your religious commitments out of the picture, as if they had no bearing on how you feel about these issues.

Should Christians Abandon Political Involvement?

It is interesting to note how the situation has evolved since the time of Acts. In the passage we are studying, it is the non-Christian Jews who try to use the power of the state against the Christians. Very soon, and for a long time, it would be Christians who would use the power of the state against Jews and people of other religions—as well as against other Christians with whom they disagreed. Christians, who had earlier suffered from the power of the state, did not learn their lesson, and simply tried to do unto others as had been done unto them. In more recent times, the power of the state has been used by people who feel that all religions are oppressive, and has therefore been used against Christians as well as Jews, Moslems, and all others.

Does this mean that the only solution is to try to regain the upper hand so that Christianity is again as influential as it once was, and we can once again use the power of the state against those who disagree with us? As you know, there are Christians who have made this their agenda and who have organized coalitions to bring it about.

If that is not the right response, should we then abandon the political arena altogether, letting it follow its own course without any input or impact on the part of Christians? Obviously, that is not the answer either. Indeed, through the centuries Christians have influenced society and its laws in ways that we would not care to lose—the abolition of slavery, laws against child labor and abuse, labor legislation, humane treatment in prisons, or international laws that seek to limit the destruction of war.

How Does the Christian Make Decisions?

The response lies somewhere between these two extremes. As Christians, we must not seek to force our religious convictions on others. Yet, as Christians, we have a view of what society should be like. We work for the attainment of that goal in the political arena. Must we not work toward that goal in ways that do not crush or destroy those who disagree with us?

On what basis do you as a Christian make political decisions? Think about some of the following options. Are they Christian? Are they in fact the ones you follow?

1. I decide on the basis of my own self-interest. Everybody else does.
2. I decide on the basis of what is best for the political party I support.
3. I decide on the basis of what is best for the nation.
4. I decide on the basis of the greatest good for the greatest number.
5. I decide on the basis of what is best for my religious group or for the church.
6. I decide on the basis of what is best for the most disadvantaged.

Dimension 4:
A Daily Bible Journey Plan

Day 1: Acts 20:7-16

Day 2: Acts 20:17-38

Day 3: Acts 21:1-16

Day 4: Acts 21:17-26

Day 5: Acts 21:27-36

Day 6: Acts 21:37–22:5

Day 7: Acts 22:6-29

Acts 19:23-41

11

*E*PHESUS

What to Watch For

We will study today an episode that took place during one of Paul's visits to Ephesus. He had been in that city earlier, but Acts tells us little about that other visit (18:19-21). All that we know is that he went there with Priscilla and Aquila, that he spoke in the synagogue, and that when he was invited to stay longer he said he had to leave, but promised to try to return. After returning to Jerusalem and then to Antioch, Paul traveled again. This time Acts does tell us about Paul's work in Ephesus, where Paul stayed for two years (19:10). As you read, be aware of the following:

➤ The event we will study took place toward the end of Paul's sojourn in Ephesus when he had already made plans to leave the city and move on to Macedonia (see 19:21 and 20:1).

➤ After two years of ministry in Ephesus, apparently the growth of the Christian community was so rapid, and the impact of its preaching so vast, that certain economic and religious interests began to worry and to take action. That is what we shall study in today's lesson.

84

1. Who instigated the riot? Why?

2. Why were the rioters so upset about Christian preaching?

3. Who stopped the riot? Why?

Paul Traveled to Ephesus

Paul had already experienced Ephesus during his previous voyage, when he went there with Priscilla and Aquila. Acts is not clear as to where Priscilla and Aquila went or how long they stayed in each place. We are told that Paul "sailed for Syria" (18:18) with them. The group made a stop in Ephesus. Paul continued to Jerusalem and eventually to Antioch. Meanwhile, Priscilla and Aquila stayed in Ephesus, where they corrected the deficient preaching of Apollos (18:24-28). Still, when Paul returned to Ephesus they seem to be no longer there, for Acts does not mention them in that connection.

A DISTURBING TRAIT

This is one more instance of a trait in Acts that may disturb those of us who wish to know the exact career of all these characters that come onto the scene and for a moment play a very important role only to disappear once again. It is a trait that shows that the basic purpose of Acts was not to tell the story of any particular person or group of persons but rather to tell the story of how the Spirit acted through these people. Thus, when someone is important in telling the story of the "acts of the Spirit," Luke brought them into the story. Once that moment had passed, Luke was quite ready to treat every character as secondary—no matter whether that character was Silas, Priscilla, or even the apostle Peter.

The Preaching of the Way Worried the Ephesians

In any case, Paul was in Ephesus, and the preaching of "the Way"—as Luke referred to it—made such an impact that people worried. Foremost among the worriers was a certain Demetrius, a silversmith who "made little shrines of Artemis" (19:24).

THE ANCIENT STATUE OF ARTEMIS

Ephesus was famous for its temple to Artemis, one of the "seven wonders" of the ancient world. Both in length and in width, it was much larger than a football field. (Today all that remains standing is a huge, single column.) In it stood the ancient statue of Artemis, which was said to have fallen down from heaven (see 19:35). In truth, the goddess who was worshiped there was not exactly the same as the Greek Artemis, but rather an ancient fertility goddess—the *Magna Mater* or *"Great Mother"*—who had been worshiped in the area from time immemorial. When the Greeks settled the area, the fertility goddess became identified with Artemis.

As happens in such cases, the temple of Artemis, besides a place of worship, was also a center of economic activity. Like many ancient temples, this one was also a bank where the wealthy could store their resources. An attraction for devotees from all over the Mediterranean world, they would come to worship the goddess and perhaps to ask her for fertility. Such pilgrims brought great wealth to the city and had become an important resource for the local economy.

Among those who made money on this ancient form of "tourist trade," were those who made little shrines of Artemis. These were reproductions that travelers could take back home, not only as a souvenir, but also as a means to renew the religious experience of their visit to the great shrine of Artemis.

In the story of the riot in Ephesus, which we are studying, Luke told us of Demetrius and other silversmiths who made such little shrines out of silver. Although no such silver little shrines have been found, archeologists have disinterred a number made out of clay. Presumably what happened was that, because silver is such a valuable metal, those who came across such a shrine made out of silver over the centuries would melt it, while those made out of clay were simply discarded or forgotten. Probably such little shrines were made of different materials, such as clay, wood, and silver. In any case, those made out of silver, obviously the most expensive, brought the most important trade.

Economic Interests and Religious Devotion

It was precisely the silversmiths, who saw their income threatened, who started the riot. Demetrius gathered the silversmiths whose business was threatened by Paul's preaching "that gods made by hands are not gods" (26). Religious and economic interests coincided: "There is danger not only that this trade of ours may come into disrepute but also that the temple of the great goddess Artemis will be scorned, and she will be deprived of her majesty that brought all Asia and the world to worship her" (27).

The final words brought back the economic issue. They subtly implied that "all Asia and the world" would no longer be coming to Ephesus to worship Artemis—and to spend its money. Obviously, "Asia" here means the Roman province by that name in the tip of Turkey, not what today we call Asia.

The result was that the silversmiths became enraged and started shouting: "Great is Artemis of the Ephesians!" (28) Were they enraged because their religion was being challenged? Or were they enraged because their income was being threatened? The text does not say. Probably both, and they themselves could not have said which.

The theater in Ephesus was a huge structure that was then under construction, whose ruins remain awesome to this day. It was built in the form of an amphitheater, as were most theaters of that time, sitting on a hillside facing the great road that led to the seaport. Its total capacity was 24,000, and it was built in such a way that whatever was said onstage could be clearly heard from any of the 24,000 seats.

The riot rapidly spilled throughout the city, and the mob moved toward the theater. Along the way to the theater, the mob dragged two of Paul's companions, Gaius and Aristarchus. Paul himself wanted to face the crowd, but the disciples as well as some "officials of the province of Asia" (31) (literally, *Asiarchs*) who were friendly to him dissuaded him.

The scene at the theater was one of utter confusion. People were gathering and shouting, but they did not really know why. When Alexander, apparently a Jew, tried to speak, the outburst became louder—presumably because the Ephesians knew that Jews did not worship Artemis: "Great is Artemis of the Ephesians! Great is Artemis of the Ephesians!" (28)

The Town Clerk Quieted the Crowd

Eventually, the "town clerk" quieted the crowd. That title did not quite express his authority. He was the link between the city assembly and the Roman government. As such, he wielded significant power; but he also had to be always mindful of Roman authority above him and of how that authority would react to whatever the assembly in Ephesus did. Thus, when he spoke, the Ephesians saw him as both one of their number and a reminder that Roman authority was always lurking behind. His speech began with words of reassurance. He declared that there was no need to create a great riot for the defense of Artemis, for after all, "who is there that does not know that the city of the Ephesians is the temple keeper of the great Artemis and of the statue that fell from heaven?" (35) In other words, why get so worked up about something that apparently no one of any consequence was denying, and that no one could deny even if they so wished?

Gods Made With Hands

Note that the mention of the goddess having fallen down from heaven was a subtle refutation of Paul's preaching, according to Demetrius, "that gods made with hands are not gods" (26).

Then he brought in an element of subtle threat: "You ought to be quiet and do nothing rash" (36). They had already done something rash! They "have brought these men [Gaius and Aristarchus] here who are neither temple robbers nor blasphemers of our goddess" (37). They had done this as if there were no law. But in fact there were laws. There were courts and proconsuls. If Demetrius and the artisans had a complaint against anyone, they should have followed proper court proceedings and not simply rioted. If it was not a matter for the courts, but something which was really bothering the Ephesians, it needed to "be settled in the regular assembly" (38) not in a riot.

Then came the final threat: "For we are in danger of being charged with rioting today" (40). The word that the town clerk employed here for *rioting* was a technical legal word, referring to a riot or an act of sedition. The penalties for rioting were severe. In extreme cases, entire towns could be wiped out! The very mention of that word by an official who somehow represented them before Roman authority, and vice versa, would have been enough to calm the ardor of the most belligerent.

Significantly, Demetrius, who was quite eloquent before the other silversmiths, did not appear eager to pursue the matter. The riot ended because, having said this, all that the town clerk had to do was dismiss the crowd. Apparently, the crowd went home quietly—perhaps even repenting for their rashness, which could have had such terrible consequences.

Dimension 3: What Does the Bible Mean to Us?

Luke the Realist

As we read this passage, what most amazes us is Luke's profound and realistic understanding of the way human minds and societies work. The picture he paints of the connection between economic and religious interests is something one seldom finds except in relatively modern authors. And yet, it has plagued religion and religious conversation for ages.

Think, for instance, of the instructions of Ferdinand and Isabella to Christopher Columbus in which they told him to pacify the natives of these lands and to bring them to the Christian faith, "so that they might be subjected to our service in peace and obedience." Or think of a letter that a leading Christian colonizer wrote to the king of Portugal. In this letter he said that the evangelization of the natives was to the advantage of the crown for, in that way, the colonizers would have more slaves to work for them. It would all result in that "Our Lord would gain many souls, and Your Majesty would receive great incomes from these lands."

Note, however, that Luke did not say that those involved in the riot of Ephesus were hypocrites. If Demetrius began with economic considerations, and if those considerations also contributed to the rage of other silversmiths, that was soon left behind in what appeared to be genuinely religious outrage that Artemis might lose some of her splendor and prestige. Likewise, Ferdinand and Isabella received the title of "Their Catholic Majesties," because they (especially Isabella) were so profoundly committed to the Christian faith.

The same is true of most of the *conquistadors*, who caused so much bloodshed in this hemisphere in their quest for gold and their simultaneous effort to "Christianize" the natives. They were sincere Christians. They thought that in what they were doing they were serving God. At their death, several of them declared that their greatest joy was that they had been able to bring so many natives to Christ!

It is important for us to realize being a sincere Christian is not enough. This thinking in turn means that, as long as we are sincere, we have no need to examine our actions or our religious commitments.

Paul Undercut the Worship of Artemis

Demetrius did not like Paul's preaching. Perhaps he convinced himself, but at least he convinced others, that the reason why Paul's preaching was to be opposed was theological: It undercut the worship of Artemis. It was true that Paul's preaching undercut the worship of Artemis. It was also true that it undercut the livelihood of the silversmiths. That was the real reason for the opposition, and the real reason for the riot.

Have you ever heard a preacher say something you may not like? For instance, about race relations, about personal morality, or about social responsibility? When you have heard such a thing, have you stopped to ask yourself the real reason why you do not like it? Is it really because it is contrary to the gospel, or is it because it goes against your interests and challenges you to change your way of life?

Luke's realism extended to the political realities that affected the way people acted and related to each other. Demetrius had some power, because he could persuade other silversmiths of his views and create a riot. The town clerk had more power. But behind the power of the town clerk stood the mighty power of Rome—and ultimately it was fear of that mighty power, communicated through the words of the town clerk, that put an end to the riot.

In this respect also Luke was realistic. When we analyze the reasons why things get accomplished or do not get done, or the reasons why some people support or oppose a particular position, we often see their immediate interests. The truth is that very often those people who we think are quite powerful are themselves serving powers and interests far higher. They in fact do not have the freedom that we think they have—and sometimes not even the freedom they think they have.

What Are the Motives for Our Actions?

What does all this mean for us and our life as Christians?

It means first of all that we must examine ourselves and try to discover the real motive for our actions. We are sinners. As such we have a large capacity for self-deception. This is one of the most important reasons why Bible study and the community of the church are so important. In them, we may hear a word that jolts us out of our self-complacency and shows that, sincere though we may be, we are not being obedient to God's will.

Then, we must learn to be "wise as serpents." Just as this passage shows that Luke was wise and understood something of the tortuous psychological and political ways of humankind, so too must we try to understand those ways, for only thus shall we be able to advance the cause of the Kingdom. Remember that Paul himself was a Roman citizen. When it was helpful to the cause of Christ, he could make use of the political power that implied. (See, for instance, Acts 16:37.)

Finally, it means above all that we must be ready to decide where our ultimate loyalty lies. Paul was a Roman citizen, and the Roman society was one of the most orderly and productive the world had ever known. Paul's respect for Rome went to the point of advising Christians to subject themselves to its authority (see Romans 13:1-7). That did not mean that his ultimate loyalty was to Rome or to its emperor—who would eventually have him beheaded. His ultimate loyalty was to Christ and to his kingdom.

Where Does Our Ultimate Loyalty Lie?

We live in the richest society the world has ever known. It is a society that offers many benefits and freedoms to its citizens. For all of that, we must be grateful. Still, where does our ultimate loyalty lie?

Dimension 4:
A Daily Bible Journey Plan

> *Day 1:* Acts 22:30–23:11
>
> *Day 2:* Acts 23:12-22
>
> *Day 3:* Acts 23:23-35
>
> *Day 4:* Acts 24:1-9
>
> *Day 5:* Acts 24:10-23
>
> *Day 6:* Acts 24:24-27
>
> *Day 7:* Acts 25:1-12

Acts 23:23– 24:27

12 *T*RIAL

What to Watch For

Paul has returned from the last missionary journey that Acts records. Watch for the following as you read:

➤ After arriving at Jerusalem and telling the church there of his missionary work and its results, Paul went to the Temple to perform certain rites of purification that took a number of days.

➤ A riot ensued with the result that Paul ended up a prisoner of Roman authorities trying to keep order. The Jewish Council then met to judge Paul's case. When the proceedings got too heated, the Roman tribune Claudius Lysias intervened. His troops returned Paul to prison, where his status was not altogether clear.

➤ Plotters schemed to kill Paul. The tribune, worried about possible disturbances and also about the safety of a Roman citizen, decided to send the prisoner off to his superiors in Caesarea so that governor Felix could decide on his fate (and also to get rid of what for him must have been a difficult situation). It is at this point that the passage we are studying picks up the action.

1. In what city does the story begin? Where does it end?

2. What is the attitude of the Roman authorities toward Paul and his preaching?

3. What is the attitude of the Jewish leaders?

4. What is the result?

Dimension 2:
What Does the Bible Mean?

Paul Was Moved to Caesarea

Roman tribune Claudius Lysias had just learned of a plot to kill Paul as he was being taken to appear once again before the Jewish Council. He decided to move Paul to a place of safety, although without committing himself by simply letting him go. Thus, he decided what government agents in similar situations have usually decided, to turn the problem over to his superiors—or, as we would say colloquially, "to pass the buck."

The exact nature of the various kinds of military forces mentioned here is somewhat in doubt. If you are interested, your teacher has more information on the subject.

In order to do that, he ordered a strong escort to convey Paul from where he was in Jerusalem to Caesarea, the seat of the Roman governor.

As a further precaution, Claudius Lysias ordered them to march at night. Doing so would make it difficult for those who saw them leave and were plotting Paul's death to make an immediate countermove.

Governor Felix Informed of the Charges

Together with Paul, Claudius Lysias sent a letter to Governor Felix in which he explained the details of the case and the nature of the proceedings against Paul (Acts 23:26-30). Such a letter (known technically as an *elogium*) was a procedural requirement when a Roman official transferred an accused prisoner to a higher court. It was a report to properly inform the higher official what had transpired before. In this particular case, Lysias presented himself in the best possible light, indicating that he had saved Paul from the rioting Jews because he was a Roman citizen—when, according to Luke's account, what actually happened was that he intervened and was about to have Paul flogged when he learned that his prisoner was a Roman citizen.

Note something of a contradiction between verses 29 and 30. In the former, Lysias said that after looking into the case, he had found that Paul "was charged with nothing deserving death or imprisonment." Then, in the very next verse, he said that he had decided to turn the case over to Felix, where he had also ordered his accusers to present their case. It is not difficult to read between the lines, and see a lesser government official who was worried that this case was too complicated for him. There were all sorts of political overtones.

The actual order of the march, as described in verses 31 and 32, is somewhat confusing. From Jerusalem to Antipatris was some thirty miles. Thus, unless they were making a superhuman effort to return to Jerusalem, it is difficult to imagine that these soldiers walked that distance overnight and then back again on the same day. Most probably what the text means is that they marched all night, arrived at Antipatris at some point in the morning, and the day after their arrival turned back to return to Jerusalem. Meanwhile, Paul and the cavalry went on to Caesarea where both Paul and the *elogium* were handed over to Governor Felix.

The Trial Began

The accusers arrived five days later. The fact that Ananias the high priest was among them shows the importance they attached to the matter. Also, they brought with them a lawyer, Tertullus, to present their case. Since there was some sixty miles from Jerusalem to Caesarea, Ananias and his party must have left Jerusalem no more than a day after hearing that Paul had been transferred to Caesarea.

The core of the trial was the two speeches, one by Tertullus and the other by Paul. Tertullus began, as was then customary, with words of praise for his audience—in this case the governor. He accused Paul of being a "pestilent fellow," and "agitator," and a "ringleader of the sect of the Nazarenes" (5) whose last crime was that he "tried to profane the

FELIX QUESTIONED PAUL

We know from other sources that Felix was a licentious and cruel man, not terribly interested in justice. This fits with his first question to Paul, asking him what province he was from. This question is not an idle one, such as might be asked upon meeting someone and asking, "Where are you from?" Felix had already been governor of Judea for some four years and would have been quite aware that religious matters in that particular province were rather thorny. Therefore, he was looking for a way to rid himself of the case. In Roman law, a criminal case could be tried either in the province where the crime was committed (in this case, Judea) or by the provincial authorities having jurisdiction over the accused.

Thus, if Paul told Felix that he was from another province, the governor would be able to rid himself of the case by having it transferred there. The problem was that Paul was from Tarsus in Cilicia, which was a free city, and where, therefore, provincial authorities had no jurisdiction. Felix had no option but to hear the case himself and to make a decision. That is why, when Paul told him where he was from, he answered: "I will give you a hearing when your accusers arrive" (35).

Meanwhile, Paul was kept in prison in "Herod's headquarters" (literally in Greek, Herod's *praetorium*), which was Herod's old palace that had become the headquarters of Roman provincial government.

temple" (6). Of all these accusations, the only ones that would interest Felix as a Roman official would have been that of being an "agitator" and of profaning the Temple—for Roman authorities had constituted themselves guardians and guarantors of the Temple. In verse 9 *the Jews*— meaning the leaders of the Council who had come from Jerusalem with Ananias—confirmed these accusations.

Note all the praise that was poured on Felix in verses 2-4, which is particularly striking because we know that Felix was far from deserving of such praise.

Then Paul began his defense. His expected commendation of Felix was very brief and noncommittal. All that Paul said to show his respect for the governor was "that for many years you have been a judge over this nation" (10). In verses 11-13, Paul denied the two serious charges that had been made against him, arguing that he did not instigate any riot as an agitator would have done, nor had he profaned the Temple. He launched into a summary of his faith and his activities, all of which would have been legal from the Roman point of view, but might serve to explain the reason for the animosity of his accusers.

Paul Remained in Custody

Two things stand out as we read this speech. The first is that Paul depicted himself as having brought alms to the poor in Jerusalem—an aspect of his ministry that is central in his letters, but which Acts hardly mentions. Secondly, and much more important, Paul spoke of the hope that he preached as a hope for the resurrection of the dead but he did not say a word about Jesus being the Messiah (or the Christ). That is understandable, for if there was one thing that a Roman governor of Judea would have feared it was Jewish nationalism, which at any point might have led to open rebellion. Since such nationalism was closely tied to the figure of the Messiah, any mention on Paul's part of the Messiah would rapidly have labeled him as indeed the agitator that Tertullus said he was.

Luke declared that Felix "was rather well informed about the Way" (22). He certainly did not mean that he was a Christian sympathizer, but rather that, having been governor of the province for a number of years, he knew what was going on. In any case, Felix decided to stall. He did this by offering the excuse that he had to wait until he heard directly from Lysias. Meanwhile, Paul remained in custody, although with some limited freedom. Friends could come, for example, and take care of his needs.

Paul Spoke of the "Coming Judgment"

Some time later, Felix saw Paul again. His wife Drusilla was with him. Since Drusilla herself was Jewish, the visit may have been more from a personal level than as an official continuation of the trial. Perhaps Drusilla was interested in hearing what this particular Jew with the new teachings had to say. Perhaps Felix wanted the advice of Drusilla, who as a Jew might have been able to understand what the controversy was all about. In any case, on this occasion, apparently Paul said more about his faith. Here he touched a raw nerve for Felix, for when he began speaking of "justice, self-control, and the coming judgment" (25), Felix became frightened and ended the interview. From what we know of Felix, it is easy to understand how he would become disturbed by hearing talk of such matters as justice and self-control and especially about a coming judgment. Here again, Luke's account of events fit perfectly with the personality of Felix as his own contemporaries described it. Again, Paul's legal status was left hanging until Felix could make a decision.

Finally, Luke added a note as to the motivations for Felix's behavior. He sent for Paul repeatedly and talked with him. Did he hope to obtain a bribe from him? In a case such as this, where the prisoner's fate was left at the discretion of a single official, it was not rare to have the matter resolved by means of a bribe. Secondly, Luke recorded that Felix kept Paul in prison for two years, and simply handed the problem over to his successor Porcius Festus, because he wanted to gain the good will of the Jews—that is, of the Jewish leaders who had accused Paul.

Paul's Attitude Toward Felix

One of the most striking features in this entire history was Paul's attitude toward Felix. Note that Felix had power of life and death over him. Yet, as one compares Paul's speech with that of Tertullus, it is evident that the latter, who only had a trial to win or lose, was much more deferential than Paul himself, whose very life was at stake. What Tertullus said about Felix was a series of lies that anyone who knew Felix would have recognized as such—probably including Felix himself. All that Paul said was that Felix had been governor for some time—which was strictly true. And later, when he was before Felix and Drusilla, he dared speak of items that he knew would be quite unwelcome by Felix: "justice, self-control, and the coming judgment."

Do we have the same Christian integrity when we deal with those who have power over us? Or do we have it even when we deal with those whose good opinion is important to us?

Will We Lose Our Integrity?

We live in a society where we are expected to be civil and polite and not disturb others unnecessarily. There is much good in that. There is also the danger that, under the guise of civility, we may lose much of our Christian integrity.

Take one example. As Christians, we believe that we are all brothers and sisters under God. We also hold that racial prejudice is bad and ought not to be countenanced. Have you ever been at a gathering where a racist joke was told about a group that was not represented there? What has been your response? Have you laughed in order to seem to be a good sport? Have you tried to act as if you did not hear it? Have you said what you actually think about racism? Those people in that gathering had much less power over you than Felix had over Paul. Those people only had the power of social convention. Did you resist those in the gathering who were laughing at the racist joke? Did you cave in?

Take a second example. Imagine someone in your town who is a rich and powerful person but does not attend church. Now suppose that one Sunday morning this person unexpectedly showed up in church. Would

97

you treat that person any differently from the way you treat any ordinary visitor? Would you be worried that saying the wrong thing or not showing enough respect would cause that powerful person not to come back? Suppose that you are the teacher in the Sunday school class this person attended. If this person said something that contradicted the very center of the gospel, would you correct him or her the same way you would correct anybody else in the class?

Paul Showed Great Patience

A second feature in this passage is the enormous patience that Paul showed. There he was, in prison for no real reason whatsoever. His Roman judge had shown that he knew that the accusations of which he was an object were specious. Yet he would not let him go. He insisted on having more interviews with him, apparently trying to elicit a bribe. Two years went by. During much of that time Paul was probably chained to a soldier. When he was not chained, he was in jail. It was a humiliating and exasperating situation that reminds one of Paul's own words in his Epistle to the Romans: "And not only that, but we also boast in our sufferings, knowing that suffering produces endurance, and endurance produces character, and character produces hope" (Romans 5:3-4).

What resources do you think Paul had to be able to live through that experience in hope? He certainly would have, as the text says in Acts 24:23, the help of friends who could come to visit him. Can you think of some others? Prayer? Scripture? Hymns?

What Are Our Resources?

What resources could you count on under similar circumstances? If you were to find yourself tomorrow in a seemingly hopeless situation without many of the physical resources and comforts to which you are accustomed, what resources do you have in your faith that would help you keep your hope alive?

Finally, this story leads us to reflect on the relationship between our Christian faith and the powers and authorities around us. The author of Acts had no illusions as to those authorities. Felix was presented as a man with little or no concern for justice and not too reluctant to take a bribe. Ananias, who was supposed to be the highest official of Jewish religion, was not very likable. Claudius Lysias brushed off his responsibility, passing it on to his superiors, and was not above slanting the story to make himself appear good.

Hopefully, the authorities in your community are much better than these. But whether they are or not, Luke's insight and realism are worthy of imitation. He did not see the church as existing in a vacuum. On the contrary, the church exists and moves within the context of these political realities—good, bad, or indifferent. Just as the early mission took place in that context, our mission today must take similar issues under account. This is not to say that we will necessarily oppose, or necessarily support, those in authority. It is simply to say that we will know they are there, understand their interests and motivations, and take them into account as we plan our mission.

Do you think a church preparing a mission statement should try to analyze the structures of power in its community? Do you think a church should try to see how these power structures relate to its mission? Luke probably would think so!

Dimension 4:
A Daily Bible Journey Plan

Day 1:	Acts 25:13-22
Day 2:	Acts 25:23-27
Day 3:	Acts 26:1-11
Day 4:	Acts 26:12-18
Day 5:	Acts 26:19-23
Day 6:	Acts 26:24-32
Day 7:	Acts 27:1-12

13

SHIPWRECK

What to Watch For

This is the last trip of Paul recounted in Acts. It eventually led him to
Rome (although that is not included in the passage we are now studying).
The trip to Rome itself was the outcome of the protracted legal process
that we studied last week. When Porcius Festus, the new governor, offered
Paul the possibility of reopening his trial by sending him back to
Jerusalem, Paul exercised his right as a Roman citizen and appealed to
Caesar. From the moment that this appeal was granted, Paul was no longer
under the jurisdiction of the governor. He had to be taken to Rome for
trial. What you are studying this week is the story of Paul's voyage to
Rome, ending in shipwreck on the island of Malta. As you read the story,
watch for the following:

➤ the subtle nuances that Luke introduced in the relationship between
   Paul and his guardians, and
➤ how that relationship developed as the story unfolds.

Dimension 1:
What Does the Bible Say?

1. Where did Paul sail from? Who was with him?

2. What was Paul's position in the ship? Did this change as the story developed? Did his authority increase or wane? Why?

Dimension 2:
What Does the Bible Mean?

Paul Set Sail for Rome

Paul and "some other prisoners" were sent together toward Rome under the custody of a centurion named Julius. Among those who accompanied Paul, not as a prisoner, but more as a companion and perhaps legally as a servant (a Roman citizen being escorted as a prisoner was allowed two servants), was Aristarchus of Macedonia, whom we met in Ephesus. Also presumably traveling with them was the mysterious narrator who told the story in the first person plural ("we"). Their first stop was at Sidon, where Julius allowed Paul to go visit his "friends"—probably other Christians. The narrator used the title "friends" because that was what Julius would have called them.

> You may wish to discuss the use of the word we during your class period.

Difficulties Began

After that the difficulties began. The winds were contrary—partially because it was late in the sailing season when the winds tended to be contrary. They were consequently forced to use Cyprus as a shield against the westerly winds and to follow the westward current that flows south of that island. Eventually they reached Myra in Licia.

There they transferred to "an Alexandrian ship bound for Italy" (6). At that time great quantities of Egyptian wheat were consumed in Rome. Therefore, the maritime traffic between Alexandria and Italy was quite active. But once again the winds proved contrary, until they finally arrived "with difficulty" (7) off Cnidus. Once again, they used the lee of a large island—in this case Crete—to protect themselves from adverse winds. Eventually they reached a mediocre port called Fair Havens on the southern coast of Crete.

At this point there was a disagreement as to what to do. It had obviously become too late in the year to continue the voyage to Rome. The question now was where to spend the winter while they waited for better sailing weather. Paul encouraged the group to remain in Fair Havens. The pilot and the owner of the ship felt that it would be better to take the chance of reaching the better port of Phoenix, some thirty miles away. The centurion took their advice. Interestingly, so did "the majority" (12). We cannot determine whether a vote was officially cast; however, human beings being human beings, it appears that opinions were shared with some "corporate wisdom" winning out. At any rate, the crew set sail for Phoenix, for which the wind, coming from the south, seemed fair.

Since the wind was from the south, they found themselves on a lee shore, and thus unable to sail out of harbor. They needed to tow themselves out with the ship's boat. Apparently that is the reason why, as we learn later, the ship's boat was at sea.

Suddenly, the wind changed. This new wind, the *euroclidon*, blew violently from the northeast. The change was so sudden that the ship could not be turned around to face it, which prevented them from being driven ahead of the wind. They could not turn, for this required presenting their side to the waves involving serious danger. All they could do was run before the wind with a sea anchor to keep the stern toward the wind and to allow steerage way—the latter absolutely necessary in order to meet the waves perpendicularly. It was not until they found themselves momentarily under the lee of the small island of Cauda that they were able to recover the ship's boat, which presumably they had been towing all along. They also took "measures to undergird the ship" (17)—a phrase on which interpreters are not in agreement. Also, they were in danger of being driven so far south that they ran on the Syrtis—a series of shoals off the northern coast of Africa that was famous as a ships' graveyard.

The Ship Was Imperiled

By the next day the ship and its inhabitants were in serious peril. They began jettisoning the cargo, presumably to make up for the weight of the water that the ship had taken in, but also because the grain would eventually swell and burst the ship open. These efforts were insufficient; eventually they had to throw overboard even the ship's tackle, including masts and sails. Even so, the storm continued unabated "for many days" (20) with skies so overcast that "neither sun nor stars appeared" (20) and the travelers lost "all hope of . . . being saved" (20).

Throughout Luke's retelling of the ordeal to this point, nothing had been said about Paul. Now, at the darkest hour, he came into the scene again with words of encouragement. He began by telling his companions that he had warned them not to sail from Crete. As we read his entire speech, we see that he was not saying "I told you so," but rather claiming that, just as he was right before in his word of warning, he was also right in offering his word of encouragement. This word came to him in a vision. An angel told him that he would not perish, for he would have to go before the emperor. Likewise all those who were traveling with him would survive. He told them that they would "run aground on some island" (26).

We are not told how the sailors and the other travelers reacted to Paul's words. How would you have reacted? Later on their fourteenth night at sea, signs pointed to the possibility that they were approaching land. They took soundings and found the bottom to be shoaling. In order not to be driven against an unknown shore at night, they cast four anchors and waited eagerly for the dawn.

A dramatic moment followed! The sailors lowered the ship's boat, saying they were going to cast anchors also from the bow—a perfectly reasonable measure to take. The first four anchors could be cast directly from the stern of the ship.

CASTING ANCHORS

The first four anchors could be cast directly from the stern of the ship. However, sailors could not cast anchors directly from the bow of the ship. They had to be cast at a distance so that a tension to counterbalance the stern anchors would be created. To do this, sailors lowered a boat, hauled an anchor for a distance, and dropped it into the sea. Then, hauling in on the various cable anchors, the ship's attitude toward wind and wave could be regulated.

Paul, however, suspected that the sailors were about to abandon ship, run for land, and leave other travelers to their own resources. The soldiers apparently believed him, for they cut the ropes and let the boat drift away.

Near Mutiny in the Face of Danger

As you can imagine, a tense situation was created in which sailors and soldiers distrusted each other (actually a near mutiny in the face of grave danger).

Just before daybreak, Paul intervened again, once more with a word of encouragement. He urged his companions to eat, promising them their lives. Interestingly in verse 35, the words that Paul used are similar to those that describe Communion: "After he had said this, he took bread; and giving thanks to God in the presence of all, he broke it and began to eat."

Paul's action elicited a response from the discouraged travelers, who responded to his words and his example by taking bread for themselves and eating. It was at this point that Luke informed his readers that the total number of sailors, soldiers, prisoners, and other travelers was 276 persons.

"In the morning they did not recognize the land" (39). Later (Acts 28:1) they learned that the land was Malta. For the present, they saw a bay with a beach, which therefore would provide an ideal place on which to run the ship ashore with a minimum of danger.

Rather than weighing anchor (which would add weight to the ship and make it run deeper in the water), they simply cast off the cables, hoisted "the foresail" (presumably the mainmast and yards had gone overboard with the rest of the tackle), and tried to reach the beach. It was at this point that Luke recorded that "they loosened the ropes that tied the steering oars" (40). Although he did not tell us before, apparently in the height of the storm when the fatigue of the sailors and the force of the storm made steering practically impossible, the steering oars had been tied in a position to keep the ship from broaching. They were untied, so as to be able to steer the ship toward the beach.

To this day the Maltese keep the tradition that this was the spot where Paul was shipwrecked. The lay of the land and the sea matches the description of Acts.

This mosaic from a floor in the Roman seaport of Ostia shows a stylized picture of a ship such as then navigated the Mediterranean. Note the steering oar that was used even in large ships instead of the more modern wheel and rudder.

They could not reach the beach. The ship hit a "reef"—more literally, a "place of two seas," meaning a shoal between the open sea and the bay. Since the bow stuck, it would appear that, the bottom was rock, not mud. Still the strength of the waves, hitting now against an immovable wooden ship, was rapidly breaking up the stern.

All Were Saved

At this point, the soldiers turned against the prisoners—including Paul, who the night before had persuaded them not to let the sailors leave the ship. They decided to kill them so that none might swim away. The reason for this decision was that a Roman soldier was responsible with his life for his prisoners. If the prisoners escaped, the soldier's life was forfeited. But the centurion, who had come to appreciate Paul and wished to save him, gave orders to the contrary. All were ordered to try for land: those who could swim, by swimming, and those who could not, with the aid of anything that might float. The result was that, just as Paul had promised, all were saved.

Paul's Novice Advice Was Good Advice

There is one element in this story that might surprise us. When they were in Fair Havens, Paul dared to give advice as to what the sailors should do. He felt they should remain where they were; otherwise they would run great dangers. The centurion and the majority of the ship's company, however, decided not to heed the advice. They felt they should yield to the pilot and owner of the ship. And with good reason! What did Paul know about ships and sailing? As far as we can tell from the New Testament, Paul knew precious little! He knew only what someone who had traveled by sea a few times might know. His advice was considered to be as helpful as that of an average airline passenger in advising a pilot and crew today! And yet events proved Paul to be right; the pilot and the owner of the ship, as well as the probably more experienced sailors who decided to go on, were proved wrong.

This experience is a common one in the life of the church today. We are living in a time of experts. Many of us seek to solve every problem by listening to the opinion of the knowledgable "consultants." There can be great value in consulting the expertise of others. If I am afraid I may have heart problems, I go to a cardiologist, not to a podiatrist. After all, the cardiologist has spent years studying the human heart and its various diseases and cures, and that ought to count for something.

The problem is that some of the more complex decisions in life and in society cannot be made on the basis of mere expertise. My cardiologist may tell me much about my heart and about adjusting my lifestyle in order to be healthier; but ultimately the question of how I am to live my life—what values it will express, what commitments it will follow—cannot be determined by my cardiologist or by any other expert.

Think now about the church and Christians trying to deal with some of the issues of our time. The United Methodist bishops issued a statement on ecological responsibility and the management of earth's resources. Immediately numerous "experts" claimed that the bishops' call ought not to be heeded. They argued that the bishops were not experts on matters of ecology and development. Another party might issue a prophetic voice of warning against the growing economic polarization of society and the need to deal with the issue of a fairer distribution of resources. Immediately there are economists whose expertise tells them that such polarization is inevitable, or that it is not really happening, or even that it is good for the economy. And, like the centurion in our story, we may decide to heed the experts rather than those who have either vision or mere common sense.

Expertise Can Be Clouded

Note that Paul recommended that the travelers not sail on the basis of common sense or vision. The "experts," that is, the pilot and the ship's owner, did not have the vision. Their eagerness to reach their goal clouded their common sense. The same is true of many of our "experts" today. We certainly do need the experts. The ship still needs the sailors, who know how to run before the wind, how to lower a sea anchor, and so on. Experts without vision, however, risk shipwreck or worse.

When it comes to some of the more complex issues of today's world—issues such as the management of earth's resources—we need the experts. But if the church has common sense (like Paul pointing out that "the Fast" was past) and adds to that a vision of God's purposes for creation, we must heed its message lest we risk individual and global shipwreck!

A second point of interest in this story is that, through Paul's faith and faithfulness, the company on board was spared. We may find this surprising, for we usually think in rather individualistic terms, and therefore tend to think that God spared Paul for the sake of his mission, and that the sparing of Paul had nothing to do with the sparing of those who happened to be aboard the same ship with him.

It is interesting to compare this story with another story in the Old Testament. Jonah was on board a ship bound for Tarshish, when a storm threatened to sink the ship. Jonah's disobedience risked not only his life but the lives of the entire company on his ship. Eventually, Jonah himself suggested to the sailors that he was the cause of their peril. He challenged the crew to throw him overboard.

Challenged to Be a Faithful and Obedient Church

These two stories lead us to think that a faithful church is itself a source of support for the world around it, no matter whether that world believes or not. Conversely, a disobedient church becomes a threat, not only to itself, but also to the rest of society, which might do well to toss it overboard!

During these last three months, we have been studying the Book of Acts. Through this study, we have learned much of what it means to be a faithful and obedient church. We have seen that, by the power of the Spirit, a faithful church is one where love leads to the sharing of resources, and where the guidance of the Spirit leads to an ever-expanding witness and mission. We have also learned that such a church will often find itself in conflict with the super-religious, who often are more interested in their religious purity than in obedience to the Holy Spirit. It also will often find itself in conflict with the rich and the powerful, who may see their position threatened. Now we learn that this conflict is a matter of life and death, not only for us as individuals or for the church as an institution, but even for the world at large. Will we have the courage and the vision to choose life?

Dimension 4:
A Daily Bible Journey Plan:

Day 1: Acts 27:13-26

Day 2: Acts 27:27-32

Day 3: Acts 27:33-38

Day 4: Acts 27:39-44

Day 5: Acts 28:1-10

Day 6: Acts 28:11-22

Day 7: Acts 28:23-31

 CTS 29?

One of the most puzzling aspects of the Book of Acts is
which it ends. The ending is so abrupt that one could al
ply quits rather than ends. If you had not read the book before, upon finish-
ing chapter 28 you would want to turn the page to find out what happens
next.

At the end of chapter 28, we are told that Paul lived in Rome for two
whole years, preaching and teaching. He still had his trial hanging over his
head. Therefore, it is only natural that a reader would ask: What happens
next? What became of Paul? Was he convicted? Was he acquitted?

There have been many theories as to why Acts ends so abruptly. It has
been suggested, for instance, that Luke wrote it while Paul was still in
Rome; therefore he simply brought his story up to the time of his writing.
There are many reasons why that suggestion is not very plausible. Among
other things, the verb tenses at the end do not match such a situation. Were
that the situation, Luke would not say that Paul "lived there for two whole
years," but rather that he "has lived there for two whole years." It has also
been suggested that, since Luke was writing to a Roman official and
wished to make Christianity appear as compatible with the civil order as
possible, he did not wish to say, for instance, that Paul was eventually
beheaded by the Roman authorities. Again, such a suggestion is hardly
convincing, for presumably Theophilus easily could have found that out,
and in that case the entire book would lose all credibility for him. It has
even been suggested that Luke intended to write a third book, but never got
around to it—a suggestion that has no other basis than the need to explain
the strange ending of Acts.

It would seem that the solution to this puzzle is in the manner in which
Luke dealt not only with Paul but also with all his other characters. They
appear and disappear in such ways that one has to conclude that Luke had a
particular reason for telling the story in such a strange fashion. At every
turn, and not just at the end, we are left wondering, "whatever became of so
and so?" Whatever happened to the other apostles whom Luke seems to forget so early in his narrative? Whatever happened to Mary the mother of
Jesus? Whatever happened to Barnabas, so important a character in the early
chapters of the book? Whatever happened to that mysterious narrator who
suddenly began to tell the story as "we"? And finally, whatever happened to
Paul?

n why Luke told his story in this strange manner is that he did
to have any of these secondary characters obscure the main char-
n his story, the Holy Spirit. Acts is not about the apostles, or about
nabas, or about Paul. It is about the Holy Spirit. And one way Luke
could make certain that we do not turn his book into a story about one of
these secondary characters was by refusing to follow the life and career of
any of them in such a way as to satisfy our curiosity. Had he continued his
book to the point where Paul died, we would be able to think that the book
was about Paul. By leaving it where he does, it is clear that the book must
be about something else—the Holy Spirit.

If the book is about the Holy Spirit, that means also that there can be no
logical end to it. One reason why we would like to see its end is that we
have grown accustomed to thinking about "the apostolic age" as a time of
great marvels, a time when the Spirit was active in the life of the church.
Thus, the end of Acts, especially if it were to continue to the death of Paul,
would be a good ending point for this "apostolic age." What Luke was
telling us, however, is that there is no such thing as an "apostolic age" in
which the Spirit is particularly active. If that were the case, once the last of
the apostles died we would have been left with nothing but their memory,
their teachings, and their inspiration. *What Luke was telling us is that all of
us, Paul as well as Theophilus and even those of us who live late in the
twentieth century, live in the age of the Spirit.* And this has not ended even
with the death of the last apostle.

That is why we could say that we are living in "Acts 29"—or, if you
wish to make room for the many other generations that have gone between
Acts 28 and ourselves, in "Acts 527." The story of Acts, because it is the
story of the work of the Spirit in the church, does not end. We are part of
it. The same Spirit, who in Pentecost made communication possible, still
today makes it possible for all of us throughout the world, in spite of our
many differences, to be one. The same Spirit, who led the church in a lov-
ing life of sharing in Jerusalem, calls us today to renewed sharing and
responsibility in the resources entrusted to us. The same Spirit, who led
Paul in his mission, leads us today in our mission. The same Spirit, who
gave Paul the vision to bring hope to a company about to be shipwrecked,
gives us today the vision to bring hope of a world at the verge of shipwreck. That is the message of Acts for us. For unto us also is the promise:
"You will receive power when the Holy Spirit has come upon you; and
you will be my witnesses . . . to the ends of the earth."

CPSIA information can be obtained at www.ICGtesting.com
Printed in the USA
LVOW04s0503030415

433065LV00002B/2/P